THE BIRTHDAY OF A NATION:
JULY 4, 1776

By FRANCES ROGERS
and ALICE BEARD

Drawings by Frances Rogers

TODAY, as we are living new chapters of United States history, it is illuminating and inspiring to re-live the history of that earlier crucial period whose basic struggle, freedom *versus* tyranny, is being repeated in our own times.

This exciting narrative takes us behind the locked doors of Continental Congress in secret session. We watch the patriot heroes — Washington, Jefferson, John and Samuel Adams, Benjamin Franklin and Patrick Henry in action as they contend, day by day, with those who would appease, and submit to tyranny. We see American towns set blazing by the enemy and American Minute Men marching to war against fearful odds. Step by step we follow the way that led straight to the Declaration of Independence.

American boys and girls will soon be building the future of America. It is an inspiration to see how it was done in 1776.

Frances Rogers and Alice Beard have proved themselves as writers of accurate and readable historical narrative through their previous books: OLD LIBERTY BELL *and* PAUL REVERE: PATRIOT ON HORSEBACK.

Button Gwinnett

John Hancock

Lyman Hall

Wm. Hooper

Samuel Chase

Geo Walton

Joseph Hewes

Wm. Paca

John Penn

Tho: Stone

Edward Rutledge

Charles Carroll of Carrollton

Tho: Heyward Junr.

George Wythe

Thomas Lynch Junr.

Richard Henry Lee

Arthur Middleton

Th Jefferson

Benja Harrison

Tho Nelson jr.

Francis Lightfoot Lee

Carter Braxton

Rob Morris   Wm Floyd   Josiah Bartlett

Benjamin Rush   Phil Livingston   Wm Whipple

Benjn Franklin   Frans Lewis   Saml Adams

John Morton   Lewis Morris   John Adams

Geo Clymer   Richd Stockton   Rob Treat Paine

Jas Smith   Jno Witherspoon   Elbridge Gerry

Geo Taylor   Fras Hopkinson   Step Hopkins

James Wilson   John Hart   William Ellery

Geo Ross   Abra Clark   Roger Sherman

Casar Rodney   Sama Huntington

Geo Read   Wm Williams

Tho M Kean   Oliver Wolcott

Matthew Thornton

The Birthday of a Nation

The Birthday of a Nation ⋆ ⋆ ⋆

JULY 4, 1776

By Frances Rogers
and Alice Beard

WITH DRAWINGS BY FRANCES ROGERS

J. B. Lippincott Company
PHILADELPHIA AND NEW YORK

January 31, 1777

"As there is not a more distinguished Event in the History of America, than the Declaration of her Independence—nor any, that, in all probability, will so much excite the Attention of future Ages, it is highly proper, that the Memory of that Transaction, together with the Causes that gave rise to it, should be preserved in the most careful Manner that can be devised."

—JOHN HANCOCK

Contents

Contents

Illustrations

The Birthday of a Nation

1

Prelude to Action

Lord Dunmore, British Governor of Virginia, was angry. From his raised dais in the Council Chamber he glowered at the group of gentlemen who stood silently attentive while his lordship pronounced sentence of punishment for their misdeeds.

The culprits, far from being disturbed or repentant, accepted the verdict without protest or denial of the charge made against them, for it was true. These gentlemen—Thomas Jefferson, Patrick Henry, Robert Henry Lee and their fellow burgesses—were being shorn of what little official authority they possessed as members of Virginia's Provincial Assembly, called the House of Burgesses.

The frowning Governor held clutched in his fist a folded newspaper. He shook it threateningly at the accused. Said he:

"I have in my hand a paper, published by order of your House, conceived in such terms as reflect highly upon His Majesty and the Parliament of Great Britain, which makes it necessary for me to dissolve you, and you are accordingly dissolved."

Which meant that until such time as Lord Dunmore

saw fit to relent (perhaps a year or more) the House of Burgesses was wiped out of existence and its present membership disorganized.

But the ex-burgesses showed no sign of regret for their wrong-doing. With dignity unruffled, they filed out of the Capitol and stepped briskly forth along the sandy road of Williamsburg to Raleigh Tavern, where they could hold discussion free from supervision of royal government—albeit without any legal power whatsoever. Free speech was not permitted in the House of Burgesses —not while Lord Dunmore was governor. A word of protest or criticism concerning the acts of King or Parliament brought prompt retribution. Lord Dunmore stopped the mouth of protest by the simple act of dissolving the House.

In the present instance the conduct of the burgesses had been peculiarly offensive to the Crown and Lord Dunmore's loyal sensibilities had been outraged.

Probably one of the things most intolerable to any high dignitary is to have a suppliant go over his head and appeal to a higher authority. And on this particular occasion the House of Burgesses had done just that.

During a previous session of the House, news of the bill to close Boston's port in punishment for the "Tea-party" had sent indignation flaming to high heaven. If the King would take such drastic measures to ensure abject obedience, where would his tyranny end? The burgesses knew that it would be useless to ask redress from the King himself, so they went over his head and appealed to Supreme Authority. A day of fasting and prayer was appointed and the House of Burgesses appealed to God.

They prayed that "the minds of His Majesty and His Parliament be inspired from above with wisdom, moderation and justice to remove from the loyal people of America all sense of danger from a continued pursuit of measures pregnant to their ruin."

Now it was customary and expected of his loyal subjects that they pray, "God *bless* the king," but to beseech God to inspire George III and his Parliament with *wisdom and justice* was clearly to imply that King and Parliament were conspicuously lacking in those qualities and sadly in need of inspiration from above. As Lord Dunmore said, it "reflected" on His Majesty and Parliament.

The prayer had been published in the *Virginia Gazette,* and it was this paper which the outraged Governor had flourished in the faces of the erring burgesses.

At the Raleigh Tavern the undaunted ex-burgesses agreed "that an attack on any one Colony should be considered as an attack on the whole."

Since Boston had been attacked, it was time for the Colonies to take united action. Therefore, let it now be proposed that all the Colonies "appoint deputies to meet in Congress" to direct "the measures required by the general interest."

This idea of a general Congress was not new. Some such plan had been discussed off and on in Boston, New York and Philadelphia, but it took the high-handed decree of Virginia's British governor to bring matters to a head.

During the early summer the Colonies, one by one, fell in with Virginia's proposal. They agreed to send delegates to Philadelphia to meet on the fifth of September, 1774.

In such wise was Continental Congress born.

2

"No Man Dares Speak of It"

I must prepare for a journey to Philadelphia, a long journey indeed!" So wrote John Adams to his wife Abigail, he being away from home on business at the time.

John Adams had been appointed Massachusetts delegate to the new Congress, and the length of the journey to which he refers as though it were a trip around the world, was the distance between Boston and Philadelphia.

John hastened to explain further:

"But if the length of the journey were all, it would be no burden."

The thing that troubled him was his fear that the gentlemen of Congress would not prove equal to the occasion. He dreaded the thought of "Congress' falling short of the expectations of the continent and especially of the people of this province" (Massachusetts).

"Great things are wanted to be done and little things only I fear will be done," he continued.

And then one can almost see John square his shoulders

and set his jaw with determination as he denounces fear and doubt.

"Vapors avaunt! I will do my duty, and leave the event. If I have the approbation of my own mind, whether applauded or censured, blessed or cursed, by the world, I shall not be unhappy."

And by bell, book and candle he meant it!

John Adams intended to deal with the problems of his country as best he might without fear or favor. Meanwhile, nothing would be gained by pulling a long face. Certainly he would enjoy meeting the fifty-odd delegates from the other Colonies who would make up the new Congress. He looked forward to good company, a fine ride and a chance to see the famous city of Philadelphia. So it was that John Adams, in a well-balanced, philosophic state of mind, joined the three other Massachusetts delegates at Tom Cushing's house in Boston.

Plans had been made for the "Committee for the Congress" (as John called it) to travel together by coach; and now on the tenth of August the narrow cobbled street in front of the Cushing home was a scene of much bustle and commotion. By the time the servants had managed to stow and strap into place the many bags and trunks belonging to the travelers, a group of interested spectators had gathered to watch the gentlemen take their departure.

The names of two of the delegates—Thomas Cushing and Robert Treat Paine—meant little to the average Bostonian, but it would have been next to impossible to find a man or woman in all the town who had not heard of John Adams and his cousin Samuel.

Sam Adams, beloved by the patriots, was cordially hated

7

by the Tories, for they believed that without his leadership there would have been no so-called "Boston Tea Party," no consequent closing of Boston's port—in short, no open rebellion against the laws of His Majesty and therefore no punishment for breaking them. Yet here—of all men—was Samuel Adams being sent to the new-fangled Congress in Philadelphia to represent the Colony of Massachusetts Bay.

The choice of John Adams, while not favored by the Tories, was at least more understandable for he was a lawyer of reputation, a man of importance.

Presently the door of the Cushing house opened and the four delegates were ushered to the waiting coach, while the curious spectators stood by all agog.

The focus of attention was Sam Adams the tax collector, who was known to be so lenient about his unpopular duty that off and on he failed to collect a workman's hard-earned money in payment of a tax. Today, as this well-known gentleman made his way to the coach, one could scarcely recognize him, so different from usual was his appearance. Sam, who never had any money to waste on new clothes and never cared a button how he looked anyway, now wore a new hat, new wig, new coat, new everything down to his new silken hose and black buckled shoes. The sight was unprecedented!

Unlike his cousin Samuel, John Adams was not oblivious to the value of a good appearance. Before taking his place with his fellow travelers, he paused to cast an approving glance at the coach and four with its mounted escort. It was well, he thought, that the members of the new Congress should make such "a very respectable parade," for their route would take them directly past Boston Common in full view of the King's troops. John hoped the Redcoats encamped on the Common might be suitably impressed by the importance of this cavalcade, despite their usual scorn for all things American. They should be, for the big coach with its four horses would be preceded by "two white servants, well mounted and well armed" while after the coach would follow "four blacks" also well mounted and elegantly clad in livery. All told, it was a sight for the eye. John settled himself with great satisfaction. And now they were off on the "long journey indeed."

After the heavy coach had rumbled through the town gate, out along the mud flats of Boston Neck and reached the mainland, the delegates found themselves forced to choose between traveling with open windows that let in clouds of dust, or closed windows that let in only the stifling heat of the sun. For more than a fortnight New England had been "burnt up with the drought" and now every blade of grass, every twig and leaf along the roadside was gray with dust. Fortunately the journey could be leisurely, with frequent stops at comfortable inns for meals, fresh horses and a good night's lodging. On Sundays the trip would be broken so that the travelers could go to church, and the industrious quill of John Adams would never fail to enter in his voluminous diary the name of the country parson, his text, and as like as not, excerpts from his long sermon.

In many towns along the route the travelers found a cordial welcome. All hail to the gentlemen of the new Congress! At New Haven their reception seemed to reach a particularly high pitch of enthusiasm.

The coach arrived about four o'clock, says John. "As

9

we came into the town all the bells in town were set to ringing, and the people, men, women, and children, were crowding at the doors and windows as if to see a coronation. At nine o'clock the cannon were fired, about a dozen I think."

Truly this was amazing and most flattering.

That night the delegates took lodgings at Bears's Tavern. Anon enter mine host, sour-faced and full of spite against all patriots, for he himself was a Tory. If his guests were puffed up with foolish vanity at their warm reception by the town, he—Isaac Bears—would quickly prick the bubble of their self-conceit. All this to-do was no personal tribute to themselves, he would have them know. There was a pack of rascally rebels in New Haven who were bound to erect a liberty pole. The arrival of the delegates with such pomp and circumstance was most opportune, for together with ringing of bells and firing of cannon, the whole show had been used by royal authority to divert the populace from erecting their liberty pole, Mr. Bears was pleased to inform the delegates.

But the gentlemen from Boston, already aware that the Tories had no liking for the new Congress, seemed less cast down than Mr. Bears had hoped. What really mattered to John was the attitude of the other delegates with whom he must work during the coming weeks. He was not any too sure just how serious were their protestations of sympathy for Boston, or how far they were prepared to go in any case. Suppose it actually came to a question of war, which delegates would side with the patriots, which with the Tories?

Naturally, every time John and Samuel Adams met one

of the delegates they kept watch to see which way the scales tipped. During the stopover in New Haven, the Connecticut delegates had made a point of calling on the Massachusetts delegates. John Adams noted with satisfaction that among the callers one at least expressed opinions that might well develop into rebellion against royal government. This man, Roger Sherman, once a shoemaker, now a lawyer, had made bold to state that "The Parliament of Great Britain has authority to make laws for America *in no case whatever.*"

If only enough delegates were of Sherman's mind, it would seem a short step to a direct and forthright demand for separation from England and complete independence for America. The "brace of Adamses" (John's term for Sam and himself) was encouraged. One must not count chickens before they hatch, but surely it was permissible to count eggs and reckon chances.

As day after day, the hot and dusty travelers made their tedious way toward Philadelphia, there was plenty of time for long and searching discussion. They would study the situation as if it lay like a map spread out before them.

The Colonies of America were in a bad way and instead of getting better, conditions were daily growing worse. King George and his Parliament were continually inventing new and unbearably oppressive laws which, if strictly obeyed, were like to reduce America to abject poverty and slavish submission. Yes, that was true. But after all, Mother England was only following an ancient precedent. The action of King and Parliament was backed by a false and mischievous theory of government.

Not England alone, but every powerful nation believed

that a colony existed primarily for the purpose of increasing the power and riches of its mother country, without any regard for the interests or happiness of the colony itself. This theory was old as the hills and just about as difficult to dislodge.

Strangely enough, even those who suffered under it were likely to uphold it as though it were a sacred commandment founded on the Gospel. Samuel Adams knew that this false commandment must be uprooted and cast out from the minds of the Colonists before America could accept the idea of independence. He himself had spent a good part of his life at the task of this very uprooting and casting out. It was his habit to talk to the common people, instilling the idea that Mother England had no God-given right to exploit her American colonies. And because Sam had met with some success in spreading his "traitorous" ideas among the populace, the Tories hated him.

John and Samuel Adams were among the very few who were already convinced that the one and only remedy for the ills that beset America was total separation from English rule. But just how difficult or how easy it might be to persuade all America to that way of thinking, the two cousins could not yet know.

The road from New Haven to New York followed along the edge of the Sound. It was always a "most miserable" road, part too soft with deep dust, or else deep mud, according to the weather, and part too hard with bumps of unyielding rock. A "most intolerable" road and the traveler must stay with it for two uncomfortable days.

At length, however, the coach from Boston reached the

SAM ADAMS SPREAD "TRAITOROUS" IDEAS

island of Manhattan and jogged down its length to New York City at its lower tip. Here, there was more visiting and sizing-up of other delegates, among them Philip Livingston who, John complains, "blusters away" at such a rate that "there is no holding any conversation with him."

John liked right well to do some of the talking himself. And besides, no man who harbored ideas of independence could listen with patience when Mr. Livingston declared that "if England should turn us adrift, we should instantly go to civil wars among ourselves, to determine which Colony should govern all the rest."

The fact that Mr. Livingston's words might hold more than a grain of truth, did not make them one whit easier to bear. Like thunderheads on the horizon they carried signs of coming storm.

John, who was never too travel-weary to keep his diary up to date, now ruefully confided to its pages the fact that he found certain aspects of his visit with the New Yorkers "very disagreeable." With the city itself he was much impressed.

"The streets of this town," he wrote, "are vastly more regular and elegant than those in Boston, and the houses are more grand, as well as neat. They are almost all painted, brick buildings and all."

Continuing their trip southward, the travelers at length came to Frankford. They had reached the last lap of their journey, for the village of Frankford was only five miles from Philadelphia. It was now nineteen days since they had left Boston: they had covered the vast distance of almost four hundred miles. A long journey indeed!

As John Adams had met and "felt the pulse" (as he put

15

it) of delegates from other Colonies, his somewhat mercurial spirits had risen or fallen according to which side said delegates seemed likely to favor. And now, on the threshold of Philadelphia, John must have been wondering what attitude Philadelphians themselves were holding toward the burning question which to him was paramount. He and his fellow travelers were not long left in ignorance on that point. They did not even have to ask; Philadelphia was telling them.

At Frankford, the travelers came upon a welcoming committee—a group of prominent citizens who had ridden out from the city to meet them.

After an exchange of polite greetings these gentlemen suggested a conference. In the words of John Adams, they "asked leave to give us some information and advice."

Now the open road was no place for such a council, so the gentlemen from Boston invited the gentlemen from Philadelphia to take a dish of tea with them in "a private apartment"—perhaps at some near-by inn, the record does not say. At any rate, the invitation was accepted and there, in the quietude and comfort of a private apartment, the welcoming committee talked at length.

The gentlemen of the committee assured the Bostonians that it could well be understood that a town in such sorry plight as Boston was at the moment—with its port closed as punishment for having dumped overboard three shiploads of good English tea—well, to be sure, in such a case, they could see that the Bostonians might (temporarily of course) be moved by a rebellious spirit toward England.

Indeed, it was even said that some among them would go so far as to be "desiring separation" from the mother country! (Heaven forbid the very thought—but there it was!)

At this point doubtless there were side glances at John Adams and his cousin Sam. Everyone knew that these two were among the chief fire-eaters of Boston. The gentle admonition continued:

"The idea of independence," said the Philadelphians earnestly, "is as unpopular in Pennsylvania and in the Middle and Southern Colonies as the Stamp Act itself."

"Now," said they, "you must not utter the word independence, nor give the least hint or insinuation of the idea, neither in Congress or in any conversation, if you do—you are undone! No man dares speak of it. You must therefore be very cautious."

In short, it was best to consider the word *independence* outlawed, outcast and effaced from the language. The Philadelphia committee left no doubt on that score.

They proceeded to disclose the fact that certain Boston Tories, sympathetic to royal government, had sent letters of alarm to friends in Philadelphia, warning them to *beware* of the delegates from Massachusetts who were, they declared, "four desperate adventurers."

So, while sipping their tea, the well-meaning committee gave timely counsel to the "four desperate adventurers," who also sipped tea and accepted the advice "thankfully."

Under the circumstances, John Adams regarded the advice as a word to the wise. "Good sense," he called it. But later he admitted regretfully that although "It dwelt deeply in my mind, I had not in my nature prudence and caution enough to always observe it." John not infrequently berated himself for his inability to keep his mouth shut. The

17

committee had in truth spoken wisely, even though their advice came like a dash of very cold water.

Presently, after tea (it must have been honestly smuggled tea) all the gentlemen again took the road and arrived in Philadelphia.

"Dirty, dusty, and fatigued" by their long, long journey (it was now the twenty-ninth of August) the four from Boston were still not too exhausted to relish the fact that about twenty-five other delegates were on hand to give them a rousing welcome and accompany them to the City Tavern.

The supper served, says John, was "as elegant as ever laid on a table."

That supper was only the first of a round of feasts. The members of the new Congress, like John Adams, were anxious to come together—they all wanted to size-up one another. Their favorite toasts were "Unanimity to the Congress," and "Union of the Colonies." All very fine but the main thing was to find out if possible the viewpoint of each delegate. Would he prove to be easy-going, or did he have a political chip on his shoulder?

The gentlemen from Boston, with the "friendly advice" still ringing in their ears, probably tried to speak with great caution. But for all that, the conservative Mr. Galloway of Pennsylvania took note of the fact that while he found their "conversation very modest," nevertheless it was "not so much so as not to throw out Hints, which, like Straws and Feathers, tell us from which Point of the Compass the Wind comes."

The first meeting of General Congress was scheduled to

"The general cry was that this was a good room," says John Adams.

But what especially delighted the gentlemen was the "excellent library" and the long entry where the delegates might walk. Wisdom might suggest a little walk now and then while they counted ten and cooled an angry passion.

Why look farther? The delegates were ready to cast their votes on the spot for Carpenters' Hall. Mr. Galloway's negative vote (he still preferred the State House) was snowed under by an overwhelming number of ayes.

Necessarily, proceedings must have been somewhat tentative that first day. A chairman (later to be known as "president") was chosen, also a secretary. As to the chairman, the delegates found that they could agree perfectly —Peyton Randolph, Speaker of the Virginia House of Burgesses, was exactly the right man for the office. But when it came to the choice of a secretary to keep the secret Journals of Congress, the members got their first taste of what was likely to happen when the conservative members did not see eye to eye with the so-called radicals.

When the name of Charles Thomson was proposed, Mr. Galloway made it quite clear that he could not endure the idea of Mr. Thomson's being given the post. Why, the man was known to be the ringleader of the radicals in Philadelphia!

Samuel Adams being present, Mr. Galloway could not say aloud, but doubtless muttered under his breath, "This Thomson is called 'The Sam Adams of Philadelphia—the life of the cause of Liberty'."

To Mr. Galloway's way of thinking, such a title was far from complimentary. But once again this poor gentleman

take place on Monday morning, September 5. No one a
that time called it *Continental Congress*. That term cam
into use a year or so later for the sake of distinguishing thi
assemblage of delegates from the provincial congresses held
by individual Colonies.

Came Monday, September 5, and also came the delegates. Here were the men and here was the time, but
where was the place? No one knew where the sessions
were to be held. So the delegates met together at the City
Tavern to discuss the question.

Mr. Galloway thought the State House the proper place,
but some of the other delegates could not agree. They said
that the carpenters had offered the use of their hall, and it
would be "highly agreeable to the mechanics and citizens
in general" to have Congress established in Carpenters'
Hall. In other words, it's well to please the people—there
are so many of them.

Then someone offered a practical suggestion:

"Why not walk over and take a look at both places? It
is not far."

Thereupon, the whole group of some fifty gentlemer
set out on a tour of inspection. They went first to Car
penters' Hall.

The building stood between Third and Fourth Street
south of Chestnut, and proved to be quite an impressir
edifice. It had been built five years earlier of import
brick laid, in a pattern of alternate black and red. The
was one large room about forty by fifty feet in size, w
twelve windows.

The first impression was most agreeable.

found himself outvoted. The radical Mr. Thomson won by a large majority.

At length, after election of officers, America's first Continental Congress was launched—slid as it were, out into an uncertain sea on its first little tryout voyage.

The Tories of Philadelphia, and many a man who did not call himself a Tory, looked askance at the locked doors of Carpenters' Hall. More than fifty gentlemen were meeting daily in secret session behind those doors of mystery. What were they doing?

Yes, what *were* they doing? They were setting out on a voyage of discovery just as truly as did Christopher Columbus. They would discover a new America, a Land of the Free. Though most of them never guessed it. Not at first.

Many of the gentlemen expected Congress to make a beeline for peace and plenty—that and nothing else—a straight way and no turnings. The delegates were cautiously determined to keep strictly in line with the course marked out for them by their respective Colonies.

But John Adams wrote, "We have a delicate course to steer."

He knew that you cannot set a course by nailing the rudder down hard and fast. The wind changes, the waves rise, there's a reef off shore. The unpredictable happens—and then what about that immovable rudder?

Only the second day after opening, when Congress had settled down to earnest but quite safe argument, suddenly into its august midst a startling rumor struck like a thunderbolt.

"Boston has been bombarded by British warships!"

"Six citizens have been killed!"

The report swept all Philadelphia.

"Who brought the news?"

"When did it happen? And why?"

No one could answer, but Philadelphia breathed a miasma of fear and reacted most strangely.

All the bells of the city (and there were so many of them) were set tolling, muffled tolling as for the dead. And while this dismal, eerie clangor shook the air, the people rushed one way and another through the streets, aimlessly, not knowing where they went nor why. They moved in dazed confusion like restless ghosts driven by despair, calling, shouting to one another:

"War! War! War!"

"Revenge! Revenge!"

It was as if some monstrous and fantastic nightmare had closed down and held the whole city under a spell of unreality, while the muffled bells tolled.

We have the description of this strange scene in letters written by the visiting delegates.

John Adams hastened to write to Abigail:

"When or where this letter will find you I know not. In what scenes of distress and terror I cannot foresee. We have received a confused account from Boston of a dreadful catastrophe. The particulars we have not heard. We are waiting with the utmost anxiety and impatience for further intelligence."

"Further intelligence" when it finally arrived made clear that the rumor which let loose Philadelphia's weird display of emotion had no word of truth in it. Boston had not been bombarded. No one had been killed.

But Philadelphia's emotional response was real enough. It must have jarred even the most stolid member of Congress—gotten on his nerves like the first warning mutterings of an earthquake.

No harm as yet . . . not yet . . . but what of later? The commoners were on alert—set at hair trigger.

3

The Brace of Adamses

The four delegates from Boston had taken lodgings in the house of Miss Jane Post on Arch Street, halfway between Front and Second Streets, a location most conveniently near Carpenters' Hall.

Well might the worthy Miss Post take pride in the fact that her new lodgers were members of the new Congress. But there is no rose without a thorn. It soon developed that one of her lodgers, Mr. John Adams, burned an appalling amount of midnight oil.

Hours after other respectable gentlemen had removed their wigs, pulled on their nightcaps and gone peacefully to bed, Mr. Adams sat writing. One could hear the scratching of his quill going on and on while one's best candles burned down to the quick, as you might say. Whatever could a gentleman find to write about at such great length?

Miss Post was not privileged to look over the shoulder of her lodger and read his voluminous diary, but we are more lucky.

During the day in Congress it was John Adams's custom to jot down notes with a lavish hand; and from these at night he would fill page on page of his diary with record of Congressional doings. To the factual record of momentous affairs was added the record of anything and everything that chanced to catch his lively and alert attention. John would tell you the facts and then he would tell you what he thought and felt about them.

In this respect he was as different as possible from his reticent Cousin Samuel. Both men seem to have been born with pens in their hands, but whereas John's quill might shed tears of ink or sputter with exasperation or fly across the page on wings of joy, Samuel's quill was disciplined to the steady and undeviating drive toward a purpose. Whether Samuel Adams himself was sad or glad his pen kept secret. His letters did not betray personal emotions nor did they ever take an occasional day off to sketch some delightfully carefree and trivial incident of daily life.

John, on the other hand, could always spare a stray glance at the passing show even while he pressed toward the great cause. He was much impressed by the "elegant" city of Philadelphia, its libraries, bookshops and taverns; and the endless round of entertainment, where the wines and food were without compare. Why, even at the homes of the "plain Quakers" one was served quantities of food: "ducks, hams, chicken, beef, pig, tarts, creams, custards" —all "fine beyond description."

Probably Samuel sat at the same table with John and ate his own share of ducks, hams, chicken, tarts, custards, etc., but you'd never catch Samuel writing it all down for posterity to enjoy long, long afterward. It would never occur to him that anyone could be interested in such mundane details; least of all would he imagine that we Americans of the twentieth century would treasure such glimpses of the daily lives of our forebears. Luckily for us, John's pen wore no shackles of reticence but ranged all over the place, free to write of anything from the pots and kettles in the kitchen to the lofty peaks of human aspiration.

John Adams was born in 1735, in Braintree, Massachusetts, not far from Boston. His father was a farmer, but a farmer who was determined that his son should have the advantage of a good education; so while John must needs do his bit at splitting wood, fetching water, feeding livestock, etc., he must also study.

But there were times when lessons became irksome and difficult and the boy balked at his task. John himself tells how his father dealt with the situation. Instead of forcing his son to study, John's father told him that if he preferred work of another sort he might drop his books. The farm needed a ditch in such and such a spot. John could dig it.

With a sense of most pleasurable relief from mental toil, John seized a spade and went to work. The inevitable followed. At first it was fun to make the dirt fly. Then, as time passed, joy began to fade and dull monotony took its place. John was bored, but still he carried on by force of determination. Ah, but presently monotony was broken by fatigue and aching muscles. Digging had become a painful job, with only pride to keep his spade at work. Long before that irritating, wearisome, backbreaking ditch was completed young John had reconsidered his aversion to books and decided that after all he would choose to study. Thereafter, Father Adams had no need to suggest a ditch as alternative to Latin grammar.

By the time John was fifteen he was ready for Harvard College.

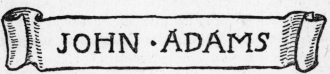

JOHN · ADAMS

During his early years this boy, like most Colonials, had been taught loyalty to England and the king. Indeed, he greatly admired George II, who was king at that time, and he felt pride in considering himself a "Britton" rather than an American. As yet there was no thought of "independency" in the mind of youthful John. He entered Harvard and in due course graduated and received his bachelor's degree. Now he must decide on a career.

While considering this question John accepted a position as Latin master in a grammar school. But that was only a way station. For a while the idea of becoming a surgeon appealed. Evidently he changed his mind on that point, for under the date August 22, 1756, he wrote in his diary:

"Yesterday I completed a contract with Mr. Putnam to study law, under his inspection, for two years."

So John Adams began the study of law. Also he began to note the nature of the laws made by king and Parliament for governing the American Colonies. Obviously, they were not overconcerned with justice, but rather with the enrichment of the mother country. John's admiration for the makers of law began to crumble. His attitude toward king and parliament suffered a change. Young John even made bold to look into the future with prophetic eyes. And although the future did not take exactly the form that he envisaged, yet there was amazing truth in John's forecast. He wrote:

"Soon after the Reformation, a few people came over to this New World for conscience' sake. Perhaps this apparently trivial incident may transfer the great seat of empire to America. It looks likely to me . . . our people, according to the exactest computation, will in another century become more numerous than England itself. . . . The only way to keep us from setting up for ourselves is to disunite us."

When John was twenty-five (1760) George II died and George III became king of Great Britain. That was a sorry day for the thirteen Colonies.

For some time past Mother England had been at war with France and too busy with her own immediate affairs to give much heed to her thirteen wayward children across the Atlantic. But now that war was over, the new king had leisure to see to it that young America was brought to book. Of late, she had been having far too much of her own way—it was high time that she should be shown the error of her ways and made to do her colonial duty toward England. His Majesty, the new king, was a firm believer in the hoary old tradition that a colony exists for the benefit of its mother country. Also he believed most profoundly in "the divine right of kings." Necessarily it followed that when a king of this despotic type began to concern himself with the affairs of America and try to bring her into line with his own ideas of dutiful and unquestioning obedience toward the Crown, there was going to be trouble.

Royal government forthwith set to work on the task of devising new and ever more vexatious rules and regulations, new and ever bigger taxes. Like ravenous birds of prey these royal measures flew across the Atlantic and settled down on the unhappy land, ready to devour both property and liberty.

Boston was the principal victim, therefore Bostonians

knew more about the cruel injustice of the new laws than did any other Colony. By 1774, John Adams's admiration for kings, and his pride in calling himself a "Britton" had long since melted into thin air and vanished.

And now, at the age of thirty-nine, John found himself a member of Continental Congress, pledged to produce a remedy for the afflictions of America. How gladly would this plump and exuberant little gentleman have proclaimed from the housetops his own sentiments regarding the cure and how difficult it was for him to restrain himself! During sessions of Congress he did succeed in keeping guard over his unruly tongue, but alas! in spite of all warning there were times when caution and prudence deserted him. Says he:

"It soon became rumoured about the City that John Adams was for Independence; the Quakers and Proprietary gentlemen [by which he meant owners of much property] took alarm; represented me as the worst of men; the true-blue-sons of Liberty pitied me, all put me under a kind of Coventry. I was avoided like a man infected with Leprosy. I walked the Streets of Philadelphia in solitude, borne down by the weight of care and unpopularity."

Cousin Samuel Adams, although as firmly convinced as John that independence was the only solution to the Colonial problem, was discreetly silent on the subject—except when he felt that his words would fall on good ground. He knew how to work under cover. For that very reason he was more feared and hated by the Tories than was John, but to all appearances he did not care.

John, on the other hand, being genial and sociable in disposition, had his sad moments when "borne down by weight of care and unpopularity." Nevertheless, judging by his diary, he was, on the whole, enjoying himself immensely. It was a most gratifying occasion when Delegate John Dickinson of Pennsylvania—who was, mind you, the very pink and perfection of conservatism—came to call on John Adams, the patriot. Drove up to the door "in his coach with four beautiful horses." John couldn't help feeling a bit flattered and hoping he had made a good impression on Mr. Dickinson. Yet it was inevitable that these two men should later be at swords' points. All the more so because both of them were so deeply sincere in their conflicting opinions.

John liked and admired many of his fellow delegates. Best of all he liked the delegates from Virginia. No other Colony had so openly supported Massachusetts, or expressed such understanding of her trials under the heel of an angry monarch. Moreover, the five delegates from Virginia displayed a fine enthusiasm. They were mightily interested in this new Congress.

Delegate Harrison, for example, said that he would have come on foot rather than not come. Quite a long walk that, since Virginia lay some three hundred miles to the south.

And Delegate Brand declared that he would have come, on this occasion, "if it had been to Jericho."

Delegate Richard Henry Lee—"a tall spare man," indeed "a masterly man" with a great reputation for eloquence—was an orator second only to Patrick Henry.

And Delegate Henry himself—that marvel of "bold, grand and overwhelming eloquence"—had, some nine years earlier, dared to outface royal government by declaring that no power on earth could take from Virginia the right to make laws for herself. Since that notable occasion he had further defied the Crown with outspoken condemnation of taxes imposed by the king. There could be no doubt concerning Mr. Henry's courage and patriotism.

But among the five Virginians the man who most of all commanded John's admiration and respect was Colonel George Washington. In fact, all patriotic New Englanders had reason to share John Adams's high regard for the Colonel.

He was a man of great dignity and reserve, not one to speak on unconsidered impulse, yet when he learned of the King's command to close the port of Boston, with intent to starve her citizens into submission, the Colonel had flung his customary reserve to the winds and declared:

"I will raise one thousand men, subsist them at my own expense, and march, myself at their head, for the relief of Boston."

John Adams said it "was the most eloquent speech, at the Virginia Convention, that ever was made."

Whether or not that gallant offer could be called "eloquent" it was at any rate self-revealing. Beneath a reserved manner Washington held in control a white-hot fire, ready to blaze up in defense of justice and freedom. And although the time for marching men had not yet come, it would come. New Englanders were not forgetting the words of Colonel Washington.

Mr. Adams fixed an expectant eye on the group from Virginia and confided to his diary:

"These gentlemen from Virginia appear to be the most spirited and consistent of any."

But if the hopeful John thought that the Virginia delegates were ready to line up with the hotheads of Boston and shout for independence right out loud, he was vastly mistaken.

Before leaving home all delegates had been instructed to lay the various grievances of their respective Colonies before Congress for consideration. And then Congress was expected to find a sure cure—but mind, a painless cure—which would be satisfactory both to the people of America and to the royal powers of Great Britain. In their instruction, every single Colony stressed its desire for harmony with the mother country.

One or two examples of the instructions will suffice to show the trend of all the others. Pennsylvania directed her delegates

to consult together upon the unhappy State of the Colonies, and to form and adopt a plan for the purpose of obtaining redress of American grievances, ascertaining American rights upon the most solid and constitutional principles, and for establishing that union and harmony between Great Britain and the Colonies, which is indispensably necessary to the welfare and happiness of both.

And even Massachusetts, where the spirit of liberty strode rampant—even Massachusetts instructed her delegates

to consult upon the present state of the Colonies, and the miseries to which they are and must be reduced by the operation of certain acts of parliament respecting America, and to deliberate and determine upon wise and proper measures, to be by them recommended to all the Colonies, for the recovery and establishment of their just rights and liberties, civil and religious, and the restoration of union and harmony between Great Britain and the Colonies, most ardently desired by all good men.

Independence? For Congress as a whole the question of independence did not even exist.

So Congress set to work trying to carry out instructions. But there was such an interminable list of grievances that presently it became evident that there must be some limitation. A resolution was therefore passed (much to John Adams's disgust): "That the congress do confine themselves, at present, to the consideration of such rights only as have been infringed by acts of the British parliament since the year 1773, postponing the future consideration of the general state of American rights to a future day."

By and large, Congress was divided into two camps. There were the conservatives who were dead set—at almost any price—on patching up difficulties with England and remaining English subjects for ever and ever.

And there were the radicals, who for the most part were reluctant about separating from the mother country, but were bound to stand by their rights, come thaw, come thunder.

Among the radicals a scattered few were already convinced that no compromise between royal government and America was possible. The choice lay between independence and slavish submission—no alternatives. With George III on the throne there could be no middle course. If America yielded passive obedience to a despot there was no knowing to what piteous depths of slavery she might descend. All the radicals could see the pitfalls, but not the mountaintops. With a few exceptions—such as John and Samuel Adams—they were not farsighted enough to look into the future and behold the miracle of development that would come to America, once she was both free and independent.

The desire for freedom was universal, but the Colonies hoped to gain freedom without separation from England. Therefore not a word was said about independence, one way or the other. Instead, Congress obediently set about trying to decide first, what were the rights of the Colonies; second, to what extent such rights had been violated by royal government. And third, just what should be done to settle these questions to everybody's satisfaction.

It was all pretty dull going.

Then suddenly, without warning, into the midst of these scrupulously discreet and humdrum proceedings came a bolt from the blue in the form of a fiery document known to history as "The Suffolk Resolves."

Paul Revere, ahorseback, came pounding down from Boston with this rash paper in his pocket.

The Resolves, drawn up by certain indignant New Englanders, breathed defiance and hot rebellion.

They declared that a king who violates the chartered rights of his subjects forfeits their allegiance.

They denounced military murders in the streets of Boston and the laws designed to shield the murderers (meaning the Redcoats).

They advised qualified citizens to use utmost diligence to acquaint themselves with the art of war, and to meet for that purpose at least once a week.

The Suffolk Resolves denounced, declared and advised at great length. Yet, even so, *they acknowledged George III as the rightful sovereign*. Which shows how difficult it was even for righteous wrath and justifiable defiance to break with the old order of things.

All the same, the Suffolk Resolves were loaded to the brim with gun-powder. They reeked of treason or patriotism—depending on which side of the fence you looked from. And this was the document laid before a Congress determined to keep to the middle way!

Yet now, there *must* be a showdown. Either Congress must approve or disapprove.

Paul Revere, ardent patriot that he was, probably spent an anxious interlude at the City Tavern, waiting . . . wondering. . . .

But sooner than would seem possible Paul was off again, galloping joyfully back to Boston with the endorsement of the Resolves.

For Congress had not been evasive. It had met the issue squarely, with the unanimous resolve "that this assembly deeply feels the suffering of their countrymen in Massachusetts Bay . . . that they thoroughly approve," etc., etc.

For the moment, at least, the gentlemen of Congress had forgotten to be noncommittal. The Suffolk Resolves had been something in the nature of a close-up—a detailed picture that brought to the delegates from other Colonies, a vivid realization of the unbearable torment of oppression suffered by the citizens of Massachusetts.

John Adams, next day, wrote to Wife Abigail:

"The esteem, the affection, the admiration for the people of Boston and Massachusetts which were expressed yesterday, and the fixed determination that they should be supported, were enough to melt a heart of stone. I saw tears gush into eyes of the old grave pacific Quakers of Pennsylvania."

Did anyone watch Samuel Adams during this highly dramatic moment?

Yes, the Tory-minded Mr. Galloway was quite sure that those "inflammatory resolves" were the work of Sam's guiding hand behind the scenes. It was no secret that Sam Adams kept express riders continually on the go between Boston and Philadelphia; and there was no question, Mr. Galloway felt, but that Sam had planned the whole event, even to the timely and dramatic arrival of Paul Revere and the Resolves.

Sam Adams was more than a little pleased with the turn of affairs. It would seem that when the Suffolk Resolves came in at the door, a certain part of Congress' predetermined caution and prudence flew out at the window. For the Resolves were conspicuously lacking in pacifism and appeasement.

As the sound of galloping hoofs receded toward Boston, along with the endorsement of the Resolves, Congress may have blinked a little, wondering at its own lapse from the straight and narrow course laid out in advance. But perhaps it was only a very little lapse—the Resolves had never once mentioned that treasonable word, independence.

Clearly, the slogan of the first Continental Congress, if put into words would read: "Go slow. Dangerous turn ahead."

Slow was the word. "Slow as snails," said John Adams. "Tedious indeed is our business. . . . Fifty gentlemen meeting together, all strangers, are not acquainted with each other's language, ideas, views, designs. They are therefore jealous of each other—fearful, timid, skittish."

John Adams, with his tireless quill, was again taking pen snapshots of the gentlemen of Congress. And indeed it would seem that many of the gentlemen sought to travel in circles forever, getting nowhere, rather than move toward that "dangerous turn ahead."

Nevertheless, the members did manage to agree on a number of measures, the most important being "the plan of the Association." Under the terms of this plan the Colonies were pledged to a policy of nonintercourse with Great Britain "until the grievances complained of should be redressed."

In other words, a country-wide boycott was to be established—a nonimportation, nonconsumption and nonexportation agreement. If England could not be coaxed into good behavior, then this drastic means of persuasion must be used, no matter how great the inconvenience to Americans.

"Let us eat potatoes and drink water," wrote John to Abigail, "let us wear canvas, and undressed sheepskins, rather than submit to the unrighteous and ignominious domination that is prepared for us."

Considering all circumstances, Congress had not made a bad start, even if it was slow.

In October, when the month was drawing to a close, the members voted to adjourn, well satisfied that they had dealt with every question "with a moderation, an acuteness, a minuteness equal to that of Queen Elizabeth's privy council." If need be—if "the grievances complained of" had not been redressed by May, 1775—a new Congress could meet in Philadelphia at that time.

John Adams no longer felt himself "sent to Coventry." Philadelphia had after all proved herself to be a most gracious and captivating hostess. He left the city in a spirit of wistful regret.

"Took our departure," says his diary, "in a very great rain, from the happy, the peaceful, the elegant, the hospitable, and polite city of Philadelphia. It is not likely that I shall ever see this part of the world again, but I shall ever retain a most grateful, pleasing sense of the many civilities I have received in it, and shall think myself happy to have an opportunity of returning them."

John Adams could not know that within a few months Destiny would roll up her sleeves, fall to and set about such an unprecedented political house-cleaning as history had never seen. And that he himself would be firmly swept back again over the rough road to Philadelphia, to do his not inconsiderable bit in the matter of getting the cleaning done and the house in order.

But even at that, Mr. Adams would gladly have done more than was allotted to him, in the years to come.

4

A Push Toward Independence

Congress had adjourned. The delegates had gone home. And not once during the session had independence been mentioned. It looked as though that glorious vision of a free and independent America might be only a dream, never to come true.

America would claim *freedom* certainly, but why claim independence?

Ardent patriots who saw the vision could shout inspired eloquence from the housetops—but men who wanted to remain Britons forever were not to be moved by eloquence. It took something more tangible than words to move them. It took bullets and blood, fire and cold steel in the hands of despotic government to make them realize that independence was necessary if they would be free.

Who knows how long a time that realization would have hung fire but for the helpful hand of George III?

Not that he meant to be helpful.

When the King sent armed forces to America, he expected them to crush out and exterminate all those troublesome ideas about freedom and independence. He expected that America would come to heel like a whipped puppy. But the King's troops produced exactly the opposite effect. Every British bullet, every British swordthrust drove America, not under the heel of royal government, but nearer and ever nearer to the bright goal of independence.

With the Battle of Lexington, April 19, 1775, came the first tryout for the King's army against the Americans.

On the little village green of Lexington, eight patriots were shot dead and ten were wounded by the Redcoats. But not one Redcoat was killed.

In our time of Gargantuan warfare, such a small incident would not even be called a battle. Yet the Battle of Lexington stands as one of the great milestones of history. Certainly not as an example of brilliant military strategy—this small skirmish was not even planned. Thomas Jefferson called it "an accident."

Both British and Americans had been instructed not to fire unless fired upon. Someone disobeyed. There was one shot and then a volley. We shall never know the name of the man who fired that first shot, nor even whether he was British or American. Paul Revere said that he himself was near Lexington Green at the time.

"One gun was fired," he says, "I heard the report, turned my head, and saw smoke in front of the troops [British], they imeaditly gave a great shout, ran a few paces, and then the whole fired."

Smoke in front of the *royal* troops . . .

At any rate, someone put his finger on a trigger and pulled.

That little act was like touching an electric button that sets in motion some vast device of untried power. The

Battle of Lexington was the beginning of one of those bitter struggles between freedom and tyranny which apparently must be fought over and again—unless (or until) the whole wide world shall someday be free and no aggressor to gainsay its freedom.

The story of the Battle of Lexington is too well known to need detailed account here. The heart and center of its importance lies in the widespread effect it had on the American people—touching even those Colonists who lived at a distance from the actual fighting.

In curtailed review, this was the way of it:

Late in the year 1773, Boston refused to pay a tax on English tea, because that tax, though small, represented the King's "right" to tax anything he pleased, regardless of justice. To pay such a tax would mean that America acknowledged and bowed down to the "divine right" of the King—which was exactly what His Majesty most ardently desired.

When the King's officials tried to force the landing of three shiploads of tea in Boston, a group of patriots boarded the ships and dumped the tea overboard. It was then that the King, in angry retaliation, had closed the port of Boston and sent British troops to Massachusetts, with orders to enforce strict obedience to all his despotic rules and regulations. The soldiers were quartered in Boston—a fact which in itself caused bitter resentment. And the King's troops, overimpressed by their little, brief authority, often abused and harassed the unhappy citizens even beyond the enforcement of their royal master's laws. For all but the Tories, life in Boston had become almost intolerable.

Such was the highly inflammable situation in the early

spring of 1775, and just at this point in the story we reach the straight road leading to Lexington.

General Gage, British Governor of Massachusetts Bay was under orders to arrest the two "rebel" ringleaders, Samuel Adams and John Hancock, who were believed to be in hiding at Lexington. The General had also learned that a quantity of military equipment had been collected by the New Englanders and stored at Concord, which was only a few miles beyond Lexington.

Here was opportunity to cut two cakes with one knife. One expedition would take care of both objectives.

Accordingly, General Gage planned to send his troops marching to Concord, where they would seize and destroy the Americans' store of guns and powder, and—since the line of march led through Lexington—the two rebels, Adams and Hancock, could be picked up as the troops passed through the village.

Now, the tactics of surprise were used in Colonial warfare even as they are today. But the curious thing about this whole incident was, that whereas it was the British who planned the surprise, it was the Americans who surprised the British—in more ways than one.

Under strictest command for silence and secrecy, in the dead of night while unwary patriots (presumably) slept, the Redcoats crossed the Charles River, where on its far shore, they found the unforeseen.

Silence? Secrecy?

The night rang with clash of bells, booming signal guns, and crackling bonfires that sent warning of danger from one community to the next throughout the countryside. Along the road to Lexington no one slept. Along that same road, well ahead of the Redcoats, had thundered a shouting horseman spreading the alarm. And where Paul Revere had passed there could be no more sleep that night. Every man, woman and child knew the "regulars" were coming. Every able-bodied man had snatched up his gun, ready for action on the minute—if it really came to shooting. But would it come to that?

At Lexington some fifty or sixty of these Minutemen had gathered on the village green. They stood there in the gray dawn, uneasily fingering their guns—*squirrel guns* for the most part, which up till now had been auxiliary to the stewpan, serving to bring down small game for the family dinner table. A different sort of hunting now.

The men grouped themselves into some show of ragged formation and waited, listening intently to instructions from their captain:

"Don't fire unless fired on, but if they mean to have a war let it begin here."

It is difficult to characterize that little homespun speech. Brave? Foolhardy? Prophetic?

Certainly prophetic. As for the rest—a sparrow standing up to a hawk—the odds between the band of Minutemen and the British troops were about in that proportion.

It was dawn when the long scarlet parade of well-drilled, well-equipped British regulars reached Lexington and came upon this absurdly small band that made so poor a show masquerading as soldiers. Major Pitcairn was in command of the Redcoats. In his opinion, America's rebellious "peasants" were not to be taken seriously. "Burning two or three of their towns will set everything to rights," the Major had declared complacently.

So, in this hoity-toity frame of mind, the Major clapped spurs to his steed and dashed forward. Addressing the odd-lot group on the green, he shouted:

"Disperse ye rebels! ye villians, disperse!"

Nobody dispersed.

"Lay down your arms!" ordered the Major.

And then, perhaps bewildered by some vague doubt of his own understanding, the Major tried again:

"Why don't ye lay down your arms?"

Why indeed? It would have been so easy to turn away and go peacefully back to their homes. They were under no compulsion to stay—except the intangible compulsion of their own convictions.

The Minutemen stood firm: —*if they mean to have a war, let it begin here. Let it begin here. . . . Do not fire unless fired on—*

And *here* it did begin, with that one anonymous shot that started the mighty engine of war.

It had not taken very long—this encounter on a village green. A trifling delay in their progress, and presently the Redcoats were back in orderly line, keeping step—right, left—on the road to Concord.

Meanwhile news of the clash on Lexington Green rang like a still alarm through outlying districts, and Minutemen came. They came, not in marching order but singly, in pairs or several in a group. Anyway they came, heading toward the smell of British gunpowder.

The Redcoats had gone on to Concord and destroyed what little stock of military supplies they could discover. Not a great deal, because Concord had been warned in time and most of the stores were well-hidden. The King's troops had missed out on another part of their errand too. Samuel Adams and John Hancock had slipped through their fingers and evaded arrest.

The day was getting on—it was time to go back to headquarters in Boston. The soldiers had been roused from their sleep long before midnight of the preceding day and were probably glad to set out on the homeward march, back along that selfsame road over which they had come earlier.

Seemingly, the way stretched clear and open before them—a peaceful, placid New England road bordered in places by low, loosely piled stone walls, the kind you still may find throughout New England. There were clumps of bushes and gnarled old apple trees, with here and there an ungainly hump of gray rock. There were tranquil farm houses, barns and quiet fields—innocent of bullets as the Garden of Eden. Or so they looked.

But as the men in scarlet started down that quiet road, bullets from unseen guns beat upon them thick as hail. To all appearances, the very stone walls, trees, rocks—everything that stood raised so much as a foot above flat earth—rained bullets.

The regulars, unaccustomed to bush-fighting, were nonplused—not knowing how to meet this outlandish method of warfare, unheard of in the old country. The Britons were brave. At first they marched stolidly on, taking an occasional potshot if they caught sight of an unwary head above the shelter of a rock, but they left an ever lengthening trail of their own dead along the way.

It is one thing to be courageous in the face of danger

known and understood, but quite another to keep your nerve when peril takes some unknown form. The Redcoats marched faster and faster. Why not? The "peasant" with his squirrel gun would not stand upright and give an honest Redcoat a fair chance to kill him—then why not hurry?

Benjamin Franklin, with a mocking gleam in his eye, described that homeward march of the British after the Battle of Lexington:

"His [General Gage's] troops made a vigorous retreat—twenty miles in three hours—scarce to be paralleled in history; the feeble Americans, who pelted them all the way, could scarce keep up with them."

Now the British expedition had not been planned with intent to kill men, but it had been planned with intent to kill Freedom. Without leaders and without weapons, the Americans would lose the power to resist royal authority, and therefore would be forced to submit to the King's will. Freedom would be dead.

And that state of submission was a thing most precious to His Majesty.

The situation in America, however, was a problem in psychology that the King and his Parliament failed to understand. Independence for America was the last thing in the world they wanted, yet every act of British violence gave America a push—not toward dependence on the approval of England—but quite the other way.

The Battle of Lexington, for example, was a push—a mighty strong push toward independence—given by what Thomas Jefferson called, "The fostering hand of the King."

5

Minutemen by the Thousand

News of the Battle of Lexington swept the country. And close on the heels of the news, like a pack of snarling hyenas, trailed savage tales of atrocity.

Every New England village for miles around had its own version of what had happened. If you were a patriot you were likely to believe a man who said, "I saw houses that had been set on fire [by the Redcoats] and old men, women and children that had been killed."

No doubt the man spoke truth. Bullets from invisible foes had rained on the King's troops as they marched back over the road from Concord. If the Redcoats saw a house that in all probability sheltered some sharpshooting Yankee, it would not be surprising if that house and every soul within it became a target for ruthless destruction. There was reason enough to believe it.

On the other hand, if you were a Tory you would believe the stories of gruesome atrocities committed (according to hearsay) by the Yankees. Wounded British soldiers had been most brutally treated! Oh, yes. Some had actually been scalped with a hatchet, even as a red savage would cut the scalp from a live man's head. In proof, a bloody hatchet had been found lying beside the martyred Redcoat.

The story concerning brutal treatment of wounded Britons was flatly denied by indignant Americans who were in a position to know the facts. Under a flag of truce, word was sent to General Gage, assuring him that all possible care was and should be taken of wounded prisoners. And furthermore, the British General was invited to send "his own surgeons" to attend them "if he had more confidence in their skill."

As for the tale of scalping: on investigation it developed that a half-grown youth had been chopping wood somewhere in the vicinity of the battle on April 19. When the startled boy was suddenly confronted by an armed British soldier the boy, having no other weapon, let fly with his hatchet. Then fled in consternation. Under the circumstances he was scarcely to be blamed.

Of course, all these ugly tales reached John Adams, who was with his wife and children at their home in Braintree. Massachusetts was seething. Men from near and far, gun in hand, were heading toward the hastily assembled army camp on the bank of the Charles River. Rumor said that living conditions in the camp were none too good. In fact, they were disturbingly bad. John Adams determined to visit the camp in person and see for himself how much truth lay behind current rumors. The safety, the very life of Massachusetts might lie in the keeping of this impromptu army that had sprung up almost over night. The welfare of these men was a matter of grave importance, and John Adams was minded to look after their interests. In this matter he would bring influence to bear on Congress. Continental Congress was scheduled to meet again in May, and John would presently be journeying to Philadelphia, for he had again been elected as a delegate.

On reaching the army camp, he found conditions quite as bad as reported.

"There was," he writes, "great confusion and distress."

The crisis had come so suddenly, there had been no time for organized preparation. Even at best, an army camp of the eighteenth century bore no resemblance to the military camps of today. When a man decided to volunteer, he need not expect to find himself well fed, warmly sheltered and smartly uniformed at public expense. Not by any manner of means!

In 1775, there was no long and elaborate preparation of or for the raw recruit. When the call came the Minuteman —generally a farmer—dropped his plough handles, picked up his gun and made off for army headquarters. That was about all there was to it. If he had spent his spare time at drill on the village green, so much the better. If time permitted, there would be further drilling in camp, but practically any man with a gun was acceptable.

After the Battle of Lexington, Minutemen by the thousand had trooped into the unpromising camp at Cambridge, where as yet there was no camp, in the sense of a place of shelter and equipment.

It was April when John Adams made his tour of inspection, and April nights in New England are bleakly cold. Yet, for most of the volunteers there was no shelter. A few makeshift tents, fewer blankets, and lucky the over-privileged man who had a chance at either tent or blanket. Sleep on the bare ground, warm yourself at your campfire and be thankful. Uniforms were the exception—a volunteer soldier could wear the clothes he came in. Arms were not standardized, any kind of gun would do, and food was likewise catch-as-catch-can. That's how it was.

Altogether it was a shabby, depressing sight, that dreary camp on the bank of the Charles River; but John Adams customarily dug beneath outward appearances. He saw "great confusion and distress," but he saw also steadfast purpose. He went home and wrote with pride:

"Neither officers nor men . . . wanted spirits or resolution."

Not having our perspective, John Adams could not know that what he had looked upon would, in time, become one of the proud legends of our country. He had seen a thing unique in history, that band of sudden warriors—America's Minutemen.

6

"Sweat and Dust and 3 Cheers"

Because of some slight indisposition—likely a cold after that trip to the army camp at Cambridge—Delegate John Adams could not start for Philadelphia along with the other Massachusetts delegates. He was obliged to delay his journey until he felt better. Then, instead of going horseback, he chose to travel in a *sulky*.

This Colonial vehicle was not like the spindly, featherweight sulky of today. Mr. Adams climbed into a contraption very like an easy chair mounted on two sturdy wheels—and they'd better be sturdy if they were to withstand the wracking they would get from the high bumps and deep ruts of an eighteenth-century road!

And thus, accompanied by a mounted servant, Mr. Adams set out for Philadelphia to attend the second meeting of Continental Congress.

It was May by now and he would ride through forests tipped with tender green, past rolling fields ploughed in rich brown furrows, past brooks dancing and chuckling in delight over being set free from ice. But it is a matter of doubt if John saw, or seeing, cared a button about the beauty of nature. He had lately seen that rough and rugged camp on the Charles River—thousands of eager patriots bravely taking potluck with come-what-might. He must convince Congress of the immediate necessity to "adopt" officially this army of New Englanders. They should become the "Continental Army."

Then too, there was the matter of a leader. The new army must have a commander in chief. If John Adams had his way, Congress would appoint the tall colonel from Virginia. By all odds he was the best choice. It might be a good chance to talk to the different delegates, one by one—buttonhole a man, so to speak, and try to make him understand that the uprising in New England was of more than local concern. . . .

And so, busy with his thoughts, Mr. Adams jogged up hill and down, through Connecticut and on to Kingsbridge, New York.

Every so often he would come upon a scene that gave further confirmation to his conviction that not Massachusetts alone, but her sister colonies also, had been caught in the swirl of warlike activities. In almost every small community along the way he was likely to see companies of men drilling on the village green. These companies might include storekeepers, blacksmiths, barbers, schoolmasters, lawyers, parsons—Jacks-of-all-trades—for now all manner of men shouldered arms and "exercised" daily, much to the delight of admiring and envious boys too young to be admitted to their ranks.

The Tories sneered and thought it a rare joke to see

YE · AWKWARD · SQUAD

their Yankee neighbors "strutting about in their Sunday Wigs with their Muskets on their shoulders, struggling to put on a Martial Countenance."

"If ever you saw a Goose assume an Air of Consequence," laughed one Tory wag, "you may catch some faint Idea of the foolish aukward, puffed-up stare of our Tradesmen."

Yes, probably they were funny. The awkward squad in its first crude fumbling is likely to be funny. But wait! Isn't there a saying, "he who laughs last . . . ?"

As the Tories were to find out presently, ridicule could not faze these determined patriots who would, in time, "make themselves masters of the essential parts of military skill."

In Kingsbridge, John Adams overtook other delegates, also on the way to Philadelphia. Among them were two now much-talked-of Bostonians, John Hancock and Samuel Adams.

In personal appearance the three Massachusetts delegates were notably different. John Adams was short and chubby of build, but full of vigor—somewhat after the manner of a stout little Shetland pony. His lean cousin towered high above him, for Sam was more than common tall.

Samuel's face was careworn and looked older than his years; so also, as a rule, did his clothes. Samuel gave so little attention to his dress that upon occasion—such as his first journey to Congress—his friends had been known to take the matter in hand and see to it that Sam Adams's wardrobe was fittingly replenished.

In sharp contrast stood forth the sartorial elegance of

young Mr. Hancock. The newly appointed delegate, John Hancock, was rich; and while no fool of fashion, he was yet something of a dandy, went in for costly clothes and wore the latest mode in wigs and waistcoats. His friends considered him "proud and touchy" but none the less a staunch patriot. It takes all kinds to make a democracy.

The delegates traveled on together. Well before they reached the city of New York, they were met by "a great number of the principal gentlemen of the place, in carriages and on horseback." The delegates, it seemed, were to be ushered into town with due ceremony and accompanied by the city militia and bands of music.

Martial music was one straw too many for Mr. Adams's long suffering mare. Here is John's account of his own narrow escape:

"It would take many sheets of paper to give you a description of the reception we found here. The militia were all in arms, and almost the whole city out to meet us. . . . Jose Bass [presumably John's servant] met with a misfortune in the midst of some of the unnecessary parade that was made about us. My mare, being galled with an ugly buckle in the tackling, suddenly flinched and started in turning short round a rock, in a shocking bad road, overset the sulky, which frightened her still more. She ran and dashed the body of the sulky all to pieces. I was obliged to leave my sulky, slip my baggage on board Mr. Cushing's carriage, buy me a saddle, and mount on horseback. I am thankful that Bass was not killed. He was in the utmost danger, but not materially hurt."

One would think that Mr. Adams too was in "the utmost danger" when his sulky "overset," but he made no comments on his own bruises. He continued:

"I am sorry for this accident, both on account of the trouble and expense occasioned by it. But in times like these such little accidents should not afflict us. . . . Our prospect of a union of the colonies is promising indeed. Never was there such a spirit. Yet I feel anxious, because there is always more smoke than fire—more noise than music."

Undoubtedly there was plenty of noise. Already thousands of spectators were lined up along the road, waiting and ready with exhilarating welcome for the delegates—especially for that now-famous pair, Samuel Adams and John Hancock, the "rebel" ringleaders who had so narrowly escaped arrest during that wild dawn of April 19.

Most of us have been eyewitness on some such occasion when a famous man is welcomed by a city. The pattern of behavior appears to be centuries old. Trumpets blare, drums beat, soldiers march, horses and carriages clatter, while the crowd jockeys for place. The people push out of bounds into the line of march for better view, and are promptly pushed back by frowning officials, but the crowd keeps on waving, shouting and cheering with heart-warming enthusiasm. There is a lot of noise and a lot of dust—smothering dust. But anyway, it's a thrilling experience if you share the spirit of it.

Elaborate plans had been made for entertaining the delegates over the week end. On the first night (May 6) the gentlemen were most properly dined and wined, and the next day they found themselves quite swamped in a round of festivities. The delegates were the social lions of the hour and all New York wanted to hear them roar, but it was more than that. New Yorkers were profoundly concerned about what had happened in Massachusetts. They wanted a detailed account. Everyone wished to know the facts concerning the Concord and Lexington affair, and they wanted the story of the escape of Mr. Adams and Mr. Hancock. Those who could not get the news first hand, took it second or third hand and then passed it along to ever widening circles of eager listeners, until every tavern in the city was agog with it.

In 1775 reliable news was not flung wide and free on the air. News was eagerly sought and hard to come by. None the less, one way or another, news found its way around.

If, for example, a man drinking his noggin of beer at the tavern was known to have been nearer than his comrades to the source of information, he was besieged with questions:

Was it true what they'd heard? "Would it have been across the sea and to the Tower of London for Sam Adams and young Mr. Hancock if the Redcoats had caught them?"

"Of a surety it was true—and with the high gallows to follow, like as not. And almost—the two gentlemen didn't get away in time."

"Why not?—with the whole countryside roused in a hubbub long before ever the regulars hove in sight."

"Why not, indeed! Because the two of them fell to arguing—that's why. Says Mr. Hancock, 'I refuse to run away—I will stay and fight.' Says Mr. Adams, 'As a delegate it's your duty to live and serve your country in Con-

gress. It's not proper to expose yourself to such a force' "
(meaning the Redcoats).

"And what did Mr. Hancock say to that?"

" 'You're wrong,' says Mr. Hancock. 'I'm right,' says
Mr. Adams. 'Wrong—right! Wrong—right!' So they
keep at it like a seesaw—getting nowhere, with time flying
and the Redcoats marching closer by the minute."

At this point the man telling the story would pause, to
prolong the moment of suspense, till his impatient listeners
urged him on.

"Ah, well—in the end Mr. Adams has his way and the
two of them drive off in Mr. Hancock's coach to Wo-
burn."

At this the listeners would be settling back in their chairs
with sighs of relief.

"But that's not all!" The narrator would whip back
the attention of his audience.

"That's not all. Belike the two gentlemen would just
be at their dinner when there's a great hue and cry—'The
regulars are almost at the door!' Then up jumps Mr.
Adams and Mr. Hancock, and no argument about it this
time. Off they rush, out of the house and make for the
swamp. Splash right into it, they do! And there they stay
hidden till danger is past."

At the thought of the elegant Mr. Hancock, safe but
wading in oozy black mire, with his silken hose and white
ruffles all besplashed—just like any homespun man might
have a bit of mud on his clothes—at such a picture, the
most ardent Son of Liberty might be permitted a grin of
amusement.

Little more than half a year had passed since the two cousins, John and Samuel Adams, delegates from Massachusetts, had traveled in company to Philadelphia—but with what a difference in the manner of their reception. Last time they had been met outside the city by that committee of warning, who, finger on lip, and side glance of suspicion, had most courteously but firmly forbidden even a whisper of the unpopular word independence.

And now it was all huzzas and beaming smiles of welcome! Every town along their route of travel from New York to Philadelphia vied with its neighbors, each trying to outdo the others in staging a spectacular reception. Ringing bells, cheering throngs and martial music—enough to deafen a man. Long before John Adams and his fellow delegates reached their destination, they were travel-worn and half smothered in the clouds of dust continually stirred up by their mounted escort.

Three miles outside Philadelphia the delegates were met by the city militia along with the inevitable band of music. "The public entry of the Boston delegates into this city was very grand," says a much-impressed eyewitness.

All most gratifying. Fatiguing to be sure, but most gratifying.

Where now were those who, so short a time since, had been ready to point a finger at John and Samuel Adams and name them "desperate adventurers"?

That night, in spite of great weariness, John must needs keep his diary up to date. He writes of being ushered into Philadelphia's City Tavern—"among Crouds of Spectators who dismissed us all smeared with Sweat and dust and 3 cheers."

Too tired to be critical of the manner of his writing, he was not too tired to rejoice in the matter of it. He had seen "strong Testimony of the Spirit and Unanimity of the people."

It could not be said that the people were clamoring for independence. Nevertheless, there was a marked change —the strong testimony of the spirit would grow and wax mighty. Give it time.

John Adams was content—for the moment.

7

The Second Congress Meets

Next morning there was no lying abed till noon for the travel-weary delegates. They must rise betimes. Congress opened at ten sharp and getting dressed was no slap-dash affair for gentlemen of the eighteenth century. Getting dressed, what with all its rather fussy details, took time even if a delegate had a servant to act as valet.

Most troublesome of all must have been the fashionable coiffure of the day. Whether a man wore his own hair or a wig, his locks were generally bepuffed, becurled and molded most skillfully into set form. Some members of Congress did not go in for elaborate hair-do's, but all of them had to shave. No gentleman of consequence allowed hair to grow on his face. Nor on his head either if he wore a wig.

In case a delegate loitered too long over making his toilet, he was sharply called to order by the booming voice of the State House bell, commanding his immediate presence in the State House on Chestnut Street. Members who were late had to pay a fine. However, all in a good cause, since the fines were turned over to charity.

This year, it had been agreed that Congress would hold its meetings in the old Colonial State House, a much finer building than Carpenters' Hall. There was a central structure of red brick, two stories high, topped by the white wooden belfry. On either side, connected by open arcades, were two smaller wing buildings. It was in the large East Room of the central building that the delegates would meet.

Whether or not tardy delegates arrived in a state of breathless haste, something of the quiet dignity of the high-ceilinged, white-paneled chamber would enwrap them and quiet their racing pulses. Inside that stately building the pace was slow.

This second Congress, with few exceptions, was made up of the same men who attended the first, the most notable addition, so far, being that wise old gentleman, Benjamin Franklin. Only a few days earlier (May 6) Doctor Franklin had landed in Philadelphia after a six-weeks' voyage from England. His return at this critical moment was regarded by everyone as most opportune. Abigail Adams, writing to John, said of Franklin:

"He must certainly be able to inform you very particularly of the situation of affairs in England."

And Abigail was right. During his long term of service in London, Doctor Franklin had indeed become well acquainted with the attitude of King and Parliament toward the American Colonies. As a result, it was not in any optimistic frame of mind that he would listen to his fellow delegates cope with the problems facing the new Congress. He had seen no rainbow of promise arching the Atlantic, one end resting securely on the British throne and the other, radiantly on Philadelphia's State House tower. Yet that, apparently, was what Congress hoped to see.

After the formal preliminaries, Peyton Randolph and Charles Thomson were reëlected President and Secretary respectively. Randolph, however, would remain in office only ten days and then return to Virginia. John Hancock would be elected President in his place.

The first subject up for consideration by the members was the recent Battle of Lexington. The bloodshed resulting from the clash between New Englanders and the King's troops was most regrettable. But, after all, was it not merely a flare up—a family quarrel—a thing to be forgiven and forgotten? Let the matter be discussed calmly and dispassionately.

Some of the delegates advocated appeasement by means of a most humble petition to His Majesty. As may be imagined, the Massachusetts members did not relish that idea.

Everyone did agree that the Colonies had the right to defend themselves. But just where defense left off and aggression began, was a ticklish question.

The whole country appeared to be bristling with guns. Everywhere the local militia was training in readiness for —for what?

Even before the Battle of Lexington, Patrick Henry had given the answer to that question while addressing the Virginia Convention. And for the next hundred and fifty years every schoolboy in America could, and generally did, recite (according to one version or another) Patrick Henry's thunderous words:

"Why stand we here idle? Our brethren are already in the field. Gentlemen may cry peace! peace! but there is no peace. The next gale that sweeps from the north will bring with it the clash of resounding arms. I know not what others may think, but as for me—give me liberty or give me death!"

The echo of that speech will never die. Even though a generation or two, living in time of peace, may smile at its old-style oratory, yet in spirit it lives—the very core and heart of America.

The "clash of resounding arms" did sweep from the north. Swift on the final words of that famous speech, hard-riding messengers pounded southward carrying news of the Battle of Lexington.

And now, in Philadelphia, while Congress was trying to find a way to rebel (with submission) and submit (with determined rebellion) all in the same breath, certain of the Colonists had taken a further plunge (all on their own) into warfare, and Congress knew nothing about it until after the whole thing was over.

It seems there was a British fort, Ticonderoga, situated upon the stream connecting Lakes George and Champlain, and the New Englanders were extremely nervous about its proximity. Suppose the Redcoats stationed there should pounce down on the unprotected farms of western New England. Naturally, after what had happened at Lexington and Concord—feelings and fears ran high. No official measures were afoot for the protection of the people, therefore some of the Connecticut men had taken matters into their own hands.

Early in the morning of May 10 (the day the new Congress opened) an ardent band of Yankee frontiersmen, known as the "Green Mountain Boys," had seized Ticonderoga. Under the leadership of Ethan Allen, the men collected on the eastern shore of Lake Champlain, preparatory to crossing over to take the fort by surprise; but owing to the difficulty of finding enough boats, only eighty-three volunteers were able to make the crossing.

That number, however, proved adequate. They found the garrison still peacefully asleep, and Allen forced the surprised sentry to lead him to the quarters of the officer in command.

The little scene which then took place has become one of the legends of history. According to Allen's own account the startled Captain Delaplace sprang out of bed, demanding by what authority he was called upon to surrender.

Allen gave the answer with gusto. "In the name of the great Jehovah and the Continental Congress!" he shouted.

So it was that the fort, well stocked with military supplies, fell to the Americans without so much as the firing of a single shot.

It took seven days for the news to reach Philadelphia. The express rider arrived late at night and promptly routed President Randolph out of bed to give him Allen's report.

Next morning, when Mr. Randolph broke the exciting news to Congress, the members "heartily cheered the enterprising Ethan Allen."

Seizing the fort was an act of self-defense, wasn't it?

Surely self-defense was different from rebellion. At least most of the gentlemen profoundly hoped it was, although certain preparations for self-defense did look remarkably like preparations for war. Still, the members should feel free to rejoice over this sudden acquisition of much-needed cannon without the slightest twinge of conscience, for Congress was not responsible for the expedition—the plan had been hatched in Connecticut.

During May, John Adams continued to keep an eagle eye on the main chance, which in his opinion—and indeed in the opinion of the other Massachusetts delegates—was preparation for the inevitable war against British tyranny.

In a letter to Abigail, John wrote:

"The military spirit which runs through the continent is truly amazing. This city turns out two thousand men every day . . . Colonel Washington appears at Congress in his uniform, and, by his great experience and abilities in military matters, is of much service to us."

Then, with a sudden burst of emotion, he added:

"Oh that I were a soldier! I will be. I am reading military books. Everybody must and will, and shall be a soldier."

But John could scarcely have had time for studying any manual of arms, let alone time for military drill. Aside from the daily sessions of Congress, there was an endless chain of committee meetings. Morover, his eyes—probably badly strained by hours of writing by dim candlelight— were now giving the unhappy gentleman considerable distress.

In June he wrote to his wife: "My eyes depress my spirits." His spirits, however, were never long in the doldrums. Before he reached the end of the letter his spirits were soaring on the wings of enthusiasm:

"In Congress we are bound to secrecy. But, under the

rose, I believe that ten thousand men will be maintained in Massachusetts . . . at the Continental expense."

Now, at last, things seemed to be shaping up, and John Adams was determined to strike while the iron was hot, by naming to Congress the man he was convinced should be given the office of Commander in chief. So John rose and spoke his mind with dramatic fervor, while at the same time, with the tail of his eye, he watched the effect of his speech on his audience.

Later on, as usual, he faithfully recorded his findings.

George Washington, John says, was at the time sitting near the door, and when he heard himself recommended in glowing terms he rose quietly and "darted into the library room."

Washington took himself safely out of range of vision. But the less fortunately placed Mr. Hancock must sit still, glued, as it were, to the presidential chair and face the music, which to him was anything but harmonious music.

John Hancock had fully expected that the high honor of appointment of Commander in chief would be bestowed upon him. When it dawned upon him that Washington, not Hancock, was the name proposed, he was for the moment taken off guard and his face gave him away.

It is to be feared that a note of mischievous glee creeps into the famous diary as Mr. Adams writes of the "mortification and resentment" expressed in the countenance of President Hancock.

These men—great men—to whom America owes so vast a debt, were no crew of bloodless, plaster saints, stalking through the pages of history like inhuman robots. Like all mortals, they must suffer in spirit the faults and failings common to the race. More honor to them that they were great *in spite* of human foibles and sensitivities.

But for the somewhat too discerning eye of John Adams, that little comedy of sentiments in Congress might have been forever lost to us. The Father of his Country "darting into the library room" to escape the embarrassment of being looked at, and the elegant President Hancock knocked off the balance of his aristocratic composure.

With such a picture before us, we are in no danger of thinking of the great men of the past as creatures that moved without deviation from the mechanical pattern of perfection, like clockwork.

Later, when the matter came up for vote, George Washington was unanimously elected Commander in chief. John Adams was so pleased that he hastened to record the good news. To John's mind, Washington had proved himself a man without compare.

He was, wrote Adams, "a gentleman of one of the first fortunes upon the continent, leaving his delicious retirement, his family and friends, sacrificing his ease and hazarding all in the cause of his country! His views are noble and distinterested. He declared, when accepting the mighty trust, that he would lay before us an exact account of his expenses, and not accept a shilling for pay."

So far, so good. But John was impatient. He and his colleagues "saw the necessity for pushing vigorous measures." At the same time, however, he realized the need for caution.

"America is a great, unwieldy body," he wrote. "Its progress must be slow. It is like a large fleet sailing under convoy. The fleetest sailers must wait for the dullest and slowest. Like a coach and six, the swiftest horses must be slackened, and the slowest quickened, that all may keep an even pace."

That letter was dated June 17, 1775. Little did John dream that on the very day, even while he was writing to Abigail, a battle was raging near Boston—a battle that would effectively rouse the "great unwieldy" America to feverish indignation and determination.

Meanwhile, down in Virginia, Thomas Jefferson, the new delegate who had been appointed to succeed Peyton Randolph, was making ready for his long trip to Philadelphia.

8

Young Man from Virginia

Thomas Jefferson, delegate from Virginia, was thirty-two years old when, in 1775, he became a member of the second Continental Congress.

The other members looked upon this new delegate with keen interest.

In personal appearance, Jefferson was a man to attract the eye. He was lean and tall—6 feet 2 inches—lithe and straight as a young Indian. His rather deep-set eyes were hazel, his hair reddish in color. In manner, he was modest, courteous and tactful. So much the gentlemen of Congress could learn at a glance. As for the real man beneath outward appearances, that was and is, even to this day, a subject for study.

In some respects, we of the twentieth century can see him more clearly than did his contemporaries, because Thomas Jefferson was so far ahead of his times. It takes a century or two to catch up with the ideas of a man of his type.

There was a world of difference in background, as well as temperament, between Jefferson and John Adams. Compare the environment of young John, the farmer's son, born on a rather small New England farm, where the sparse and rocky soil must be coaxed and toiled over before it would yield its reluctant crop; with that of Jefferson, son of a rich man, inheritor of acres by the thousand in the lush and fertile lands of Virginia, where white servants and black slaves were so numerous that a gentleman need never do a hand's turn of manual labor—what a contrast of background! Yet these two men would be working together, yoked by the same great cause; and in the future they would be close friends.

When little Tom was only five years old, he began going to school. And since anything approaching the idea of a kindergarten, to smooth the hard road to learning, was still far in the future, the child must have hit the alphabet of knowledge head on, with no sweet and flowery paths of ease to soften the impact. But he could take it, without the alternative lesson of ditch digging, for he loved books.

At nine, the boy was sent to a more advanced school where he began the study of Latin, Greek and French, languages in which he later became proficient. During this period, Tom lived with his family at Shadwell, the Jefferson homestead, and life seems to have jogged along in normal, pleasant ways for the schoolboy until he was fourteen. Then came a tragic shock. His father, Peter Jefferson, died, leaving him in a predicament peculiar to the times.

According to the custom of the day, the eldest male was considered head of the family. Tom was the oldest boy, therefore he became head of his family, consisting of his widowed mother, six sisters and a baby brother.

Notwithstanding the fact that guardians for him had

THOMAS · JEFFERSON

been appointed by his father, they apparently gave him little or no direction except when he asked for it. Young Thomas continued his schooling, but for the most part, he was left to his own devices, with freedom to follow wherever inclination led. And Tom only fourteen!

It may be that even at that early age, the boy began to have some perception of the fact that freedom does not mean permission to follow any passing whim, without responsibility as to where it may lead. Later in life he wrote of his all-too-sudden self-responsibility:

"When I recollect that at fourteen years of age, the whole care and direction of myself was thrown on myself entirely, without a relation or friend qualified to advise or guide me, and recollect the various sorts of bad company with which I associated from time to time, I am astonished I did not turn off with some of them and become as worthless to society as they were."

Perhaps nowhere else on earth were there such alluring temptations to spend a life "worthless to society" as our southern Colonies presented. Even while Jefferson was growing up, the celebrated hospitality of the South was in full swing. Groups of young people—house parties—were lavishly entertained for days on end, first at one Colonial mansion and then at another. There were sports, games, dancing, fine clothes, rich food and drink, and servants by the score in attendance so that a man need not so much as stoop to buckle his own shoe.

At that time, even as now, the South was famous for its fine, highly bred horses. The gay young blade, astride his mettlesome horse, could sweep like the wind wild and free as a centaur, across that matchless land with no bar-

77

riers to stop him, except those of nature, such as a virgin forest or unfordable water.

The possession of fine horses naturally led to horse racing and fox hunting. Cock fighting, at that time, was a sport within the law, and not only was it tremendously popular with the commoners, but also very fashionable among the gentry.

And there was gambling—extravagant, ruinous gambling.

For the wealthy young man of Virginia life could so easily, so temptingly be all play and no work. No wonder Jefferson was astonished that he did not turn off with his bad companions.

It was not because he had no taste or aptitude for the pleasures of youth. He was a magnificent horseman and good at "manly exercises," he enjoyed games and sports and liked dancing with the lovely daughters of the South as well as the next young man. Gaiety tempted him—he confesses as much—but he allowed himself no excessive indulgence, because there was in him an inherent urgency to press on beyond the bounds of superficial pleasures.

Jefferson was by nature an avid student. One of his friends wrote of him that he could "tear himself away from his dearest friends, and fly to his studies."

He seems to have been worried by the constant demands on his time made by visitors to Shadwell. In writing to one of his guardians he explained that as long as he stayed "at the Mountain [Shadwell] the Loss of one-fourth of my Time is inevitable, by Company's coming here and detaining me from school."

Tom Jefferson determined to go to college. It was no

uncommon thing for the young men of his social standing—sons of rich planters—to go abroad for their education, but Tom elected to stay in his own Colony and go
to the College of William and Mary in Williamsburg,
Virginia's capital.

When the sixteen-year-old Tom took his preliminary
examination for entrance, he was already so far advanced
in his studies that he was able to skip the first two- of the
four-year course. At nineteen he graduated, but continued
to study his chosen profession, the law, in Williamsburg.
So that for five years after graduation, he still enjoyed the
peculiar privilege which that unusual place presented;
namely, the privilege of meeting and making friends with
most of the outstanding men of the day.

Williamsburg was by no means a city. It was small, yet
in character very unlike the usual small town or village.
Periodically this early capital of Virginia blossomed forth
with all the gaieties of metropolitan life. For the rest of
the time it went to sleep like the dormouse.

There was a main street, about three-quarters of a mile
long, running straight through its center, with the College
of William and Mary at one end and the capitol building
at the other. There were only about two hundred houses,
most of which were unoccupied a good part of the season.
But at intervals, there were what contemporaries called
"Publick times," when the Provincial Assembly and
Courts of Law were in session. Then it was that Virginia's
capital awoke with a start to find itself all suddenly trans-
formed into a metropolis in miniature.

At such times, the dust rose whirling from its unpaved
roads as brightly painted coaches, accompanied by scores

of mounted servants, ploughed up the sun-baked sand. Burgesses, lawyers, men of importance were coming to town. And not the men alone, but also the ladies of their families, together with unstinted trunks and boxes. Best bibs and tuckers, finest feathers and furbelows would be on parade in the capital. Then the locked and deserted houses flung wide their doors and windows and came to life with a bang. The social season was on. There was dancing and feasting and gaiety galore. No young student at the college could be expected to keep his nose in a book under such circumstances—and young Jefferson was no exception to the rule.

Close at hand was the Raleigh Tavern, now extravagantly brilliant with the light of a hundred candles, extravagantly brimming over with pretty girls, ravishing in their voluminous ball gowns. Music, youthful laughter and the appetizing fragrance of rich food wafted through the tavern windows, for Raleigh Tavern was used as a center for most of the entertainments. Tom Jefferson was not for wasting opportunity by staying outside its hospitable doors. He laughed and danced with the best of them.

In his student days, Tom spent many a gay and carefree evening at this same Raleigh Tavern, where years later, he would sit in solemn conclave with his fellow exburgesses after Governor Dunmore had dissolved the House and dismissed its members with a reprimand. But as yet the mighty burden of America's destiny sat lightly on his young shoulders.

He was interested in governmental affairs, but there were so many other interests in life. Jefferson loved music, and according to report, played extremely well that most difficult instrument, the violin. He loved architecture. Indeed as an architect he was highly gifted. Even while in college he began plans for the building of his famous residence at Monticello.

During the five years while he was studying law with that conscientious thoroughness which characterized the man, he yet found time to travel a bit, going north to have a look at those two famous seaports, Philadelphia and New York. In a letter written at the time, Jefferson gives an excellent picture of the difficulties encountered by the Colonial traveler.

"Surely never did a small hero experience greater misadventures," he writes, "than did I on the first two or three days of my travelling. Twice did my horse run away with me and greatly endanger the breaking my neck on the first day. On the second I drove two hours through as copious a rain as I have ever seen, without meeting with a single house to which I could repair for shelter. On the third in going through Pamunkey, being unaquainted with the ford, I passed through water so deep as to run over the cushion as I sat on it, and to add to the danger, at that instant a wheel mounted a rock which I am confident was as high as the axle, and rendered it necessary for me to exercise all my skill in the doctrine of gravity, in order to prevent the center of gravity from being left unsupported, the consequences of which would, according to Bob Carter's opinion, have been the corruition of myself, chair and all into the water."

A year after this adventurous trip north, Jefferson, at the age of twenty-four, was admitted to the bar. For some years thereafter his career was that of the successful lawyer.

But whether or not he himself knew it, all through the various stages of his life and education—Jefferson as schoolboy, as college student, as law student and finally as full-fledged lawyer—Jefferson, the *statesman* was growing and developing.

Even as a boy, he tells us, "I paid attention to what went on in the legislature." As a college student he often walked to the far end of the sandy main road to listen to the fiery debates in the House of Burgesses. Some of them "most bloody," said he.

Probably the most dramatic scene witnessed by the young law student came at the moment when he, listening to "torrents of sublime eloquence from Mr. Henry," heard the famous climax of the speech protesting against the Stamp Act. Patrick Henry, after summarizing "those examples of successful resistance to oppression which made glorious the annals of Greece and Rome" had dared approach the dangerous peak of supreme defiance.

"Caesar," he cried, "had his Brutus, Charles his Cromwell and—" with a pause to let his tense audience fearfully anticipate the next example of downfall, "—George the third—" A voice from the audience shouted, "Treason! treason!" but Henry went on, "may profit by their example. Sir, if this be treason, make the most of it."

It was becoming increasingly obvious to Thomas Jefferson that the fusty laws of the past could not give true answers to current problems of America. His analytical mind was ever busy testing by principles of truth and justice the questions debated in the House of Burgesses. In the spring of 1769, he himself became a burgess, eager to take an active part in the discussion of affairs affecting not only Virginia, but all thirteen Colonies; for he knew that the strained relations between England and America touched every Colonist in the land.

At his first opportunity Jefferson introduced a bill to make it lawful for slave owners to free their slaves. Except under special conditions the freeing of slaves was against the law, and Jefferson himself could not free all the slaves he had inherited. His bill, however, was too far in advance of the times. It did not pass.

The following year, Jefferson came upon adventure and misadventure in his private life. In February, his home at Shadwell burned to the ground and his entire library was destroyed. Writing to a friend, he said:

"On a reasonable estimate I calculate the *cost* of the books burned to have been 200 sterling. Would to God it had been the money, *then* had it cost me never a sigh."

Fortunately the buildings at Monticello were sufficiently advanced to give shelter to him, his mother and sisters.

Some two years later Jefferson met Martha Skelton, daughter of a lawyer friend, and fell in love. The lady was beautiful, charming, intelligent and something of a musician. The young suitor asked nothing more except her consent, which she gave. So they were married and (one would like to say) lived happily ever after—indeed, as far as mutual affection and congenial tastes were concerned, they did. But Martha was not strong and her devoted husband was often harassed by anxiety about her health.

In 1774, when the ex-burgesses had urged the meeting

of a "general Congress to consult upon the present state of affairs," Jefferson was convinced, at that time, that royal government had not the slightest intention of being just and fair in its dealings with the Colonies. On this point he writes:

The "long series of oppressions begun at a distinguished period too plainly prove the deliberate, systematical plan of reducing us to slavery."

The King and his Parliament had repeatedly taken steps that could lead only to absolute control of America's way of life, regardless of her long established rights. The *rights* of British America.

Jefferson had indeed made a profound study of that subject. He had reached certain conclusions regarding the fundamental rights of mankind, and the relation between a Colony and the mother country. He was resolved to make a statement of the truths that were so evident to him. But Jefferson was no orator. His most effective medium of expression was not his voice but his pen. He excelled in the power to make clear in written words the truths that he so passionately believed.

Therefore, in the summer of 1774 he set himself the task of writing a paper which, in brief form, would present the rights of British America. In it, he suggested that Congress should send an address to King George III, and then went on to outline the form and substance of such an address.

Jefferson's paper was a most amazing blend, beginning with courteous words and continuing with ruthless meaning—ruthless, that is, in respect to the King's vanity and self-conceit. As an example of the iron fist in a glove of chiffon velvet this famous paper would be hard to beat.

First, His Majesty was to be told exactly what he was. And second, he would be told what he had done, and next, what he ought to do. To quote Jefferson's own words, he proposed that a "humble and dutiful address be presented to his Majesty, begging leave to lay before him as Chief Magistrate of the British Empire, the united complaints of his Majesty's subjects in America." It was "humbly hoped" that the address "penned in the language of truth and divested of those expressions of servility, which would persuade his Majesty that we are asking favors, and not rights, shall obtain from his Majesty a more respectful answer," etc.

The King was invited to reflect that he was "no more than the chief officer of the people, appointed by the laws, and circumscribed with definite powers, to assist in the working of the great machine of government, erected for their use, and, consequently, subject to their superintendence."

Then followed a long list of the acts of royal government and a most unflattering judgment of those acts. Jefferson wrote in the long, decorous, well-turned phrases of the scholar and statesman. If his "Summary View" of rights were put into the colloquial terms of the common man, it might read something like this:

"Look, George III. There is nothing superhuman about a king. You are only a servant employed by your subjects to do a certain job for them. We, your Colonial subjects, call your attention to this fact and ask you to come down off your high horse and attend strictly to business.

"Here is a list of the bad laws that royal government has put over on Colonial America. We ask you to repeal these laws and give us back our rights. And don't imagine you would be doing us a *favor*. We ask *rights*, not favors—it is your plain duty to give them to us.

"Are you going to do it? We have asked you before, but you did not answer. Now please answer."

Stripped of the transparent velvet of Jefferson's decorous wording, you have the iron fist of a meaning that hits straight and hard at the mark. Too straight and hard—that was the trouble with it.

Because of illness, Jefferson was unable to attend the Virginia Convention and present his paper to the members. So he made two copies, one of which he sent to Patrick Henry, the other to Peyton Randolph, chairman of the Convention.

What Patrick Henry thought of the paper—whether he approved or disapproved, Jefferson could only guess, for Henry never mentioned it. Later, Jefferson wrote, "Mr. Henry probably thought it too bold as a first measure."

Seemingly, the members as a whole also thought the paper "too bold."

"Tamer sentiments were preferred," wrote Jefferson, "and as I believe, wisely preferred: the leap I proposed being too long as yet, for the mass of the citizens."

Undoubtedly, the mass of the citizens, whose backing was necessary to Congress, still held in a kind of almost religious awe the title of king. Jefferson's lack of reverence for His Majesty, George III, would have shocked them deeply.

At its root, the idea of a king's *divine right* reaches far back into the dim past, when a powerful ruler was thought to be a god and was reverenced as such. For example, Alexander the Great considered himself a god. Of course as time went on, belief in the divinity of rulers faded out. No longer was a king looked upon as actually divine, and yet—because of the reluctance of the human mind to investigate the truth or falsity of a long cherished tradition —some trace of the idea, unreasoned but vaguely felt, still remained, especially among the less intelligent. To flout the divine right of George III—was not such a thing akin to sacrilege?

In America, it was necessary to tear down and weed out this superstition before the people as a whole could accept the idea of breaking away from allegiance to the king, or see their right to claim independence. The change must come, but gradually.

Jefferson's paper, although not accepted by the Virginia Convention, was not destined for the discard. Several of the "author's admirers" saw to it that *A Summary View of the Rights of British America* was printed in pamphlet form. And although the "Summary View" was considered too forthright in 1774, it is interesting to note how it foreshadowed the entirely forthright Declaration of Independence, written a little less than two years later.

On the eleventh of June, 1775, the newly elected delegate to the second Continental Congress started on his way from Virginia to Philadelphia. Jefferson traveled in a phaeton, accompanied by his colored servant, Richard, riding postilion. Nowadays one could journey to the opposite side of the globe in less time and with less difficulty.

From Jefferson's account book we learn various little details of the long journey. There was a short stop in Fredericksburg to buy a postilion whip for Richard, and a new horse for the master. Next day a guide was hired— a wise precaution to keep the travelers on the right road —for most of the roads were mere wheeltracks, with never a signpost to point the way. A stranger was in grave danger of taking the wrong turning or fork, and then finding himself miles off his course before discovering his mistake.

In Annapolis, Jefferson could not resist dropping into a bookshop to pick up a few more books. Next day he reached Wilmington, Delaware, where the first guide was replaced by another. And on June 21, the phaeton from Virginia was joggling its bumpy way over the uneven cobblestones of Philadephia's main thoroughfare.

9

The Olive Branch Petition

June 21, 1775—the day delegate Jefferson reached
Philadelphia—found the Quaker City peacefully
concerned with normal affairs of the moment and
still blissfully unaware that the British and Americans had
fought a bloody battle in Massachusetts. What little commotion there was in town probably centered around plans
for giving the new Commander in chief, George Washington, a festive send-off on his way to camp.

Arrangements were being made for an impressive procession with a band of music, "a large troop of light horse
in their uniforms," and a long line of "well-wishers" following in carriages—among the latter would be John and
Samuel Adams.

There was no hitch in the proceedings. On the morning of Friday, the twenty-third, General Washington and
his escort rode through streets lined with admiring spectators. Outwardly all was as it should be, according to plan,
and the General was the very picture of calm dignity. But
those in touch with Congress realized that the General's
mind could not have been as composed as his appearance
would suggest.

For on Thursday, at twilight, a disturbing message had reached President Hancock—a message all too brief, too exasperatingly indefinite. There was word of a battle at "Bunker's Hill," but no details—nothing, in fact, by way of dependable news. John Adams, greatly worried, wrote to his wife of "a report which distresses us almost as much as that we had last fall of the cannonade of Boston . . . We wait to hear more particulars. Our hopes and fears are alternately very strong."

Here we have an example of the slow pace of communication in former times:

On June 17, 1775, the Battle of Bunker Hill was fought only a few hundred miles from Philadelphia. Yet it took six days for a messenger, riding at top speed, to carry the news to Congress; whereas in 1941, when Pearl Harbor was attacked, it took not days, not hours, but only minutes for the news to girdle the whole earth.

It was late Saturday night when the official messenger from Cambridge pounded into Philadelphia, and set the quiet streets echoing between darkened houses where early-to-bed citizens were peacefully dreaming. But there were men still lingering in the Coffee House, where presently the report of the fight on Breed's Hill was read aloud. The news was definite this time, but hard to believe.

"The British won?"

"Our men lost?"

"Yes, that's the report, but listen how it was! The New Englanders gave ground only because they ran out of powder. . . ." Thus by word of mouth the news was spread.

Twice the British had charged up Breed's Hill. Twice

they had been met by such a hot rain of lead as even the veterans of European wars had never known. Their shattered ranks were driven back with staggering losses.

The British did not lack bravery but this was plain slaughter, for the New Englanders had first marked the English officers, picking them off like rabbits, leaving the troops bewildered and disorganized.

By old-world standards the men of New England knew little enough of soldiering, but life-long practice in gunning for small game had made them superb marksmen. According to a grim saying of the time, they could shoot the nose off a man's face at a hundred and fifty yards. Chances are, very few Yankee bullets missed their mark that day.

But when, for the third time, the British charged up the hill, they met no rain of lead because the Americans had no more powder. For lack of ammunition the patriots must needs give way and let the King's men take the hill —Breed's Hill it was, yet that battle has ever since borne the name of the connecting hill—Bunker Hill.

The Redcoats had won, but they had bought victory at such an appalling price in British lives that the victory was more like defeat. And the English knew it. Said one officer, "One more such victory and there would not be a King's man left to carry word of it back to England."

The Tories now had occasion to reconsider some of their erstwhile impressions. Those ridiculous mock-soldiers, the Yankees, who so comically drilled on village greens, sending one into fits of laughter—perhaps, on second thought, they were not so funny after all!

On Monday morning, a serious-minded group of men sat in the big East Room of the State House and listened to the official report of the battle.

The outlook was not reassuring. Without predetermined intention on the part of America *as a whole*, these hostile encounters kept happening one place and another. First Lexington and Concord, then Ticonderoga, and now Bunker Hill. The menace of war was like a fire which, once started, flings its brands far and wide till all the land is in danger of being swept by one great conflagration. Would it be possible to extinguish the firebrands one by one before the flames spread farther? And how was this to be done?

Some of the delegates were for hurriedly collecting all the gunpowder Philadelphia could spare and immediately sending it off to Cambridge, in the hope that if only the Americans had enough powder, they could drive out the invaders once for all.

Other members of Congress held back, warning their colleagues against hasty action. As yet England knew nothing about the Battle of Bunker Hill. It would be wiser, said the cautious ones, to wait and see how the King and Parliament received the news, wait and find out what *they* were going to do about it. Possibly they would "recede."

Presently letters concerning the battle began pouring into Philadelphia. Citizens in its vicinity had climbed to the rooftops, or the summits of neighboring hills, and watched the progress of the fight. They had seen Charlestown in flames—"the church steeples making great pyramids of fire above the rest." A "parcel" of British shells had set the town's nine hundred wooden houses ablaze—a terrible thing to see.

To John Adams came a letter from his home in Braintree. Abigail wrote:

"The day—perhaps the decisive day—is come, on which the fate of America depends. . . . How many have fallen, we know not. The constant roar of the cannon is so distressing that we cannot eat, drink, or sleep."

A few days later she wrote again. Eager to learn what effect the news of the battle was having on Congress, she asked John:

"Does every member feel for us? Can they realize what we suffer? And can they believe with what patience and fortitude we endure the conflict?"

John answered, "No. They can't. They don't."

Thinking that direct news from Boston was good propaganda which might be used to prod laggard Congress into quicker action, John Adams had already seized the opportunity to hold forth, gruesomely describing for Congress "the groans and cries of the infuriated and oppressed." But it was no good. His audience was polite but unimpressed.

"Congress," he complained, "is not so much alarmed as it ought to be."

Perhaps for the moment Mr. Adams had forgotten his picturesque similies of a large fleet sailing under convoy whose rate of progress must be kept in balance between the fleetest and the slowest. The delegates, no matter what their personal opinions might be, must still be held in check by the decisions of their respective Colonies.

Not even the new delegate, straight from the progressive

Colony of Virginia, was authorized to make a plea for united defiance of the mother country.

Jefferson's pamphlet, *A Summary View of the Rights of British America* was already well known to Congress. It had been handed about, read and commented on by the members. John and Samuel Adams, together with other progressives, judged it excellent, but even the patriots could see that the time had not yet come for such plain speaking.

Jefferson had been cordially welcomed by his colleagues in Congress. This gentle, courteous, modest gentleman from Virginia, would never bluster and outshout a man of differing opinion. Indeed he scarcely spoke during the regular session. Day after day, he would sit listening, himself in complete silence, while all about him raged argument and debate, until the very walls of the Assembly Chamber might well be set quaking like the walls of Jericho.

Later, John Adams, in writing of Jefferson's reluctance to join in public debate, said that throughout Jefferson's term as a delegate he had never heard him "utter three sentences together" from the floor of the House.

But there are more ways than one in which to convey ideas, and the young Virginian was known to have "a happy talent for composition." Indeed it was said that he "wielded the most elegant pen in America." There would soon be opportunity to wield that pen.

Within a week after first taking his seat Jefferson was appointed to serve on a committee whose business it was to draw up an official statement setting forth America's reasons for taking up arms. One attempt to write such a statement had already been made—the original committee, it seems, had written one draft, but Congress had not liked it. What was needed was a paper that General Washington could read to the troops, a paper that would rouse and inspire the fighting men. Would Mr. Jefferson try his hand at it?

Mr. Jefferson would and did. His paper bristled with statements as uncompromising as a row of bayonets: *Nothing is so dreadful as voluntary slavery . . . We fight not for glory or conquest. We fight in defense of the freedom that is our birthright. . . .*

And then he submitted his draft to his fellow committeemen.

Now one of the committee was that same John Dickinson of Pennsylvania, who had so politely called on John Adams. Mr. Dickinson was the leader of the conservative group in Congress. Trust John Adams to note the appearance of the gentleman. He describes him as "tall, but slender as a reed; pale as ashes."

It is not difficult to imagine the expression of consternation on that ash-pale face as Mr. Dickinson's eyes traveled across Jefferson's paper, taking in the ringing and dauntless sentences written by the courteous, modest gentleman from Virginia.

Mr. Dickinson was shocked! Such wording was far too harsh. . . . Surely Mr. Jefferson must realize how unwise it was to use language so "strong."

Mr. Jefferson made no protest. He said that he would gladly turn his paper over to Mr. Dickinson to soften as much as he saw fit.

Mr. Dickinson, nothing loath, proceeded to soften the

statement by the simple method of throwing out all but the last few paragraphs of Jefferson's draft, and then writing a brand new paper himself.

The final statement proved a satisfactory compromise. The conservatives liked what Mr. Dickinson had written; John Adams and his group liked Jefferson's spirited paragraphs, few as they were.

A year must pass before the conservative members of Congress and the American people at large, slowly inching their way, would come to the realization that there was no smooth and flower-strewn road to freedom. A year, and then Jefferson would write a document with no trace of "softness"—a document wherein the "facts" would be "submitted to a candid world" in the form of a Declaration of Independence.

But in July of 1775, a good part of Congress was still bent on placating King George. It voted to send him one final petition, but a far different kind of document from that suggested by Jefferson in his *Summary View of the Rights of British America.* This was to be an "Olive Branch Petition," by way of an invitation to consider that the stormy flood of dissension should now ebb and depart. Naturally, Mr. Dickinson was the man who could be trusted to deal softly and gently with this delicate overture, so he was directed to prepare a draft of the petition.

What Thomas Jefferson thought about Mr. Dickinson and his petition is a matter of record.

"He was so honest a man," wrote Jefferson, "and so able a one that he was greatly indulged even by those who could not feel his scruples. . . . Congress gave a signal proof of their indulgence to Mr. Dickinson, and of their great desire not to go too fast for any respectable part of our body, in permitting him to draw their second petition to the king according to his own ideas, and passing it with scarcely any amendment. The disgust at its humility was general; and Mr. Dickinson's delight at its passage was the only circumstance which reconciled them to it. . . . He could not refrain from rising and expressing his satisfaction and concluded by saying 'There is but one word, Mr. President, in the paper of which I disapprove, and that is the word *Congress*.' On which Ben Harrison rose and said 'There is but one word in the paper, Mr. President, of which I approve, and that is the word *Congress*.'"

Mr. Dickinson was so anxious to appease King George. And since the King would never admit that any such unauthorized body as Congress even existed, why antagonize His Majesty by dragging in that word *Congress?* asked the cautious Mr. Dickinson.

But on this point only, the worthy Mr. Dickinson was not permitted to have his way. The obnoxious word was not crossed out.

As for John Adams, the whole idea of sending a petition to the King filled him with disgust. Mr. Dickinson's humble phrases seemed to him not only futile but ridiculous. In a flurry of temper John wrote to a friend that a "piddling Genius, whose fame has been trumpeted so loudly, has given a silly Cast to our whole Doings."

Although nowhere in his letter did John Adams mention Mr. Dickinson by name, it was perfectly obvious that the "piddling Genius" could be none other than the writer of the Olive Branch Petition. The exasperated Mr. Adams was just cautious enough to leave this letter unsigned, but still not cautious enough. Taking another sheet of paper, he wrote to his wife, and this letter he signed with his initials, *J. A.*

Then both letters were neatly folded, addressed, and given to young Ben Hitchbourn (Paul Revere's cousin) who was returning to Boston, and glad to do a favor for Mr. Adams. Ben would act as postman.

Probably that would have been the end of the matter except for a most unlucky happening.

The British authorities had a way of stopping a traveler and relieving him of any private papers or letters which promised to be of interest to royal government. And it was while he was crossing a ferry at Rhode Island that Ben ran afoul of some British officers.

Without more ado, the unofficial postman was obliged to hand over all the letters in his saddlebag, and the King's men found their search rewarded. There were two letters which interested them mightily. One, addressed to Mrs. John Adams was signed *J. A.*; the other, though not signed was clearly written by the same hand. It took no bright detective to guess the author—the worst of it was, both letters contained references to plans then under consideration in Congress.

Writing (as he fondly thought) only for the eyes of his wife and of a close friend, Mr. Adams further put himself on record as advocating a scheme "to arrest every Friend to [royal] Government on the continent" and hold them "as Hostages for the poor Victims in Boston."

With the idea of getting John Adams into hot water with "every Friend to Government" (the Tories), the British decided to make the two letters public. They also hoped to start quarrels among the members of Congress. To this end the letters were printed in Boston; also copies of them were sent to England to be published in *Lloyd's Evening Post*, so that all good Englishmen could see "the real intentions of those Miscreants who have misled his Majesty's subjects in North America to commit acts of open Rebellion."

Needless to say, Mr. Dickinson soon knew exactly what John Adams had written about him. And next time the two gentlemen met on the street John Adams was to experience the cut direct.

In the vain hope that the whole unfortunate incident might be overlooked by Mr. Dickinson, Mr. Adams removed his three-cornered hat with a flourish and favored the approaching Mr. Dickinson with a courtly bow. But alas! John Adams was to find himself "passed haughtily by." Mr. Dickinson's stock of humility had run out.

The ashen-pale countenance of that gentleman may have become noticeably red, but he managed to convey his injured feelings without so much as a glance at the embarrassed and conciliatory Mr. Adams.

John later confided to his diary the sad conviction that "we are not to be upon speaking terms nor bowing terms for the time to come."

On that day neither man knew the fate of the petition to the King which Mr. Dickinson had penned with such meek and loving care.

Weeks must pass before a ship could bring the humiliating news that the Olive Branch Petition had been spurned, scorned, disdained and utterly ignored by His Majesty. In short, the King would not even look at it. Nor would he consent to see the loyalist, Mr. Penn (acting as dove), to whom Congress had entrusted the delivery of the Olive Branch Petition.

In vain had the earnest Mr. Dickinson striven to express a humble attitude. It mattered not at all whether the challenging word *Congress* were left in or taken out.

10

Knocked About the Ears

The Olive Branch Petition had to cross the sea eastward in a sailing vessel, and then report of its fate had to cross the sea westward—likewise in a sailing vessel. That would take months, and not until November could Congress find out how the King had received their olive branch.

Meantime, in August, Congress had adjourned for a brief rest. But by the middle of September most of the members were back in Philadelphia.

Waiting for word from the King caused a kind of stalemate. Benjamin Franklin described it as an odd state, neither in peace nor war, neither dependent nor independent. As usual Congress pulled two ways. The less "forward-looking gentlemen" wanted nothing done that would close the "Door of Reconciliation." According to their ideas, if only matters were handled tactfully, without harsh words, the unhappy "dispute" between the mother country and her colonies would be peacefully settled.

The word *dispute* roused the ire of John Adams. He said, "War it is, so let it be called war." And he hated the terms *colony* or *colonies*—such words smacked of Mother England's apron strings. "Far better," said John, "to substitute *state* or *states*." As for the olive branch, he had no faith in it. Like Patrick Henry, John Adams would guide his feet by the lamp of experience and judge the future by the past.

Judging by the past, could anyone expect George III to listen to reason or a plea for justice? As well expect the leopard to change its spots.

By September, 1775, American Colonists were ready to "dye Free-men rather than live slaves," but all the same, on the question of independence they continued to stall and put off final decision. And of course Congress mirrored this indefinite attitude.

Nevertheless, by now it had become obvious that the little dispute with England would need guns and soldiers to carry on the argument. So, with great enthusiasm and plentiful lack of knowledge and experience, Congress plunged into the tremendous task of preparing for war. No matter how little the delegates knew of the larger principles of warfare, they could deal copiously with minor matters. They could invent endless small rules and regulations—red tape by the mile. No time-taking detail seemed too trifling, complicated, or tedious for their attention.

As Ben Harrison wrote to General Washington, "The Gentlemen could not think of parting with the least particle of their power."

Long hours were devoted to discussions concerning food for the soldiers, before Congress could agree that on a Monday a soldier should be given one pound of beef, one pound of turnips or potatoes, and one pound of bread;

while on a Tuesday, he would receive the same fare with the addition of pudding.

Maybe pudding as a boost to morale was important, but not that important. John Adams, for one, found it difficult to give his full attention to the culinary subjects under discussion. He felt that warships not puddings should be the prime subject for consideration. He himself, having been born and bred on the coast was acutely aware that all coastal towns along the Atlantic lay exposed and defenseless—easy targets for the first enemy ship that chose to destroy them. For not one of the thirteen Colonies owned a single man-of-war!

But the delegates from inland were not impressed by danger to the coast, and at first they did not take seriously John Adams's plea for armed ships. He found it difficult to convince them of any such necessity.

At length, however, Congress—although lukewarm about it—did yield to persuasion and appoint a naval committee. The committee recommended the fitting out of "two swift-sailing vessels." Only *two*, that far would they go and no farther.

But in October, the King's navy produced an argument far more convincing than anything John Adams could say about the need to guard the coast line.

There was a little town called Falmouth, located on the coast of Maine where Portland now stands. Early in October the town had been ordered by the British to hand over its cannon, small arms and ammunition, but like other New England towns Falmouth lacked that submissive spirit so dearly desired by His Majesty, and Falmouth refused to hand over anything.

The royal order was repeated, along with a threat "to deliver or be beat about the ears." Again the town refused—and in consequence, took her beating. The British warships stood safely off shore and shelled Falmouth into flaming ruins, without the slightest risk to themselves.

Falmouth of course had no way whatsoever of defending herself. Yet British General Howe was "proud" to report to Parliament the destruction of five hundred buildings. The town put the loss at one hundred and fifty buildings—but that was bad enough. October weather was bleak, and in a small community even a hundred homeless families can create a serious problem.

From the standpoint of royal authority, shelling the town was good discipline—an example that went to show what would happen when royal orders were disobeyed. Falmouth had been disobedient.

The indignation of Congress, when news of the destruction of Falmouth reached Philadelphia, was unanimous this time. Not even the most ardent supporters of the Crown could find a good word to speak in behalf of such ruthless measures. Instead of producing a state of terrified submission, the news stepped-up the plans for an American navy —Congress decided to double the fleet. The Continental navy should consist of *four* vessels instead of *two!*

Thus would slow-moving Congress take one more little step in the name of self-defense. But it would continue to turn a deaf ear to all John Adams's pleas to stop beating about the bush and have done with talk of "the dispute" with the mother country. Dispute indeed!

By way of making bad matters worse came reports of

serious trouble brewing in Virginia between the royal governor, Lord Dunmore, and the patriots.

The Governor, thinking to aid His Majesty's cause by obliging "the rebels" to stay home on their plantations "in order," as he tactfully put it, "to take care of their families and property," had issued a proclamation offering freedom to all slaves and indentured servants who volunteered to serve under the King. A clever scheme that. A man deprived of his servants would of necessity be far too busy at home to have any time for plotting rebellion—or so thought Lord Dunmore.

The royal Governor probably thought exceeding well of his diplomatic scheme for staving off rebellion, but it was not original. In the old country, laws and conditions had from time to time been specially designed for the sake of preventing men from meeting together and plotting against despotic government. Lord Dunmore doubted not that the old plan would continue to be successful.

But matters did not work out as the Governor expected —something was wrong with that scheme when applied to Americans.

Instead of being hampered by his proclamation, the rebellious Virginians gained new strength. Their ranks were suddenly enlarged by numbers of erstwhile loyalists, who now deserted the King and cast in their lot with their fellow countrymen. The disillusioned Virginians stampeded the recruiting centers. "Give us rifles, ammunition and a chance to even up the score," they demanded.

As for the slaves, the Governor's promise of freedom did cause a number of them to flee to British headquarters in Norfolk. But not all of the runaways managed to get there, for many were picked up on the roads and carried back to the plantations by force.

Nevertheless, the proclamation did succeed in creating considerable disturbance. One letter, reaching Philadelphia by express from Virginia, described conditions in that Colony.

"The flame runs like wildfire through the slaves, who are more than two for one white in the Southern Colonies," said the writer. "The subject of their nocturnal revels, instead of music and dancing, is now turned upon their liberty. I know not whence these troubles may lead us."

Neither did Lord Dunmore.

The Governor's reputation for fair dealing was already *nil*, and now his lordship's courage likewise vanished. His "palace" in Norfolk was well fortified, but he and his family fled the town and took refuge on a royal man-of-war anchored off shore. Even there, under protection of royal cannon, he felt none too safe, so he ordered a fort to be built at the southern entrance of the town, where a bridge crossed the Elizabeth River.

The fort was a visible dare. But the Virginian patriots, undaunted, managed to build for themselves a breastwork on the opposite side of the river. And there, with only the river and the fort between them and Norfolk, the patriots took their stand.

On a dark night, early in December, the threatened action began. Some two hundred Redcoats, accompanied by a large band of Tories and Negroes, set out from Norfolk. They reached the fort at half-past three. It was still pitch dark and uncomfortably chilly, so food was passed around while British gunners, under command of Captain Squire, made ready to begin the attack with two pieces of cannon.

Then, when the moment was right, the King's men started valiantly across the narrow causeway toward the rebel camp.

They were in high spirits. Says one of the royal officers: "We marched up to their works with the intrepidity of lions. But, alas! we retreated with much fewer brave fellows than we took out. Their fire was so heavy, that, had we not retreated as we did, we should every one have been cut off."

The Virginians, it seemed, were as expert marksmen as their Northern cousins, the New England Yankees. Moreover, the Southerners had entrenched themselves most cleverly. All but surrounded by a treacherous swamp—a water-covered, muddy trap draped with thick entangling vines—the patriots faced the causeway over which only six of the enemy could advance abreast.

The British were courageous but they hadn't a chance.

By seven o'clock that night the King's little army had had more than enough of it, and all those who were able to retreat, did so as fast as their weary legs could carry them back to Norfolk and onto the royal ships.

Since the road to Norfolk was now wide open, the triumphant patriots without more ado marched in, took possession of the town; and by way of bravado, fired a "salute" of small arms at the royal *Otter*.

Next morning men from the *Otter*, their feelings badly ruffled, rowed ashore with a grim ultimatum:

"If one more shot were fired in the direction of His Majesty's ship, the impudent rebels could expect the town to be knocked about their ears."

There it was again. "Knocked about the ears"—a sinister phrase.

The coastal town of Falmouth had already suffered that violent form of discipline. But Norfolk was still defiant; and Lord Dunmore, as might have been expected, played the tyrant's trump card; namely, terrorism.

All tyrants, past and present, have believed that if only the people were sufficiently frightened, they would fall to their knees in abject submission. George III believed it, and so did many of the men to whom he gave official power in America. Fear—that was the thing—spread paralyzing fear throughout the American Colonies and royal government would thereafter work its will, smooth as silk and no trouble at all.

Accordingly, Lord Dunmore was doing his best to further this desirable state of terror. In the South, Norfolk should be an example as had Falmouth in the North.

About four o'clock on New Year's Day the cannonade began. And the patriots, under direct fire of three royal ships of war, were soon driven from the wharves. Thereupon royal boats were landed, and sailors with flaring torches set fire to wooden buildings all along the water front.

It was said that at a given signal, the King's men had set fire to houses, tanyards, windmills, churches, etc., "all so quick you couldn't tell which burned first."

Once started, there was no checking the flames that went roaring, crackling, spreading through the whole town, gaining more strength with everything they devoured. The people had been driven to the Back Country and were in great distress. They had fled for their lives,

NORFOLK·IN·FLAMES

many of them not daring to stop long enough to snatch up their most precious possessions—or even necessities, for that matter—not so much as a blanket for protection against the cold night. Even Captain Chesholm (American) and his family had been forced to take shelter in the woods; but the Captain was luckier than most because he had succeeded in getting hold of a tent for his family to live in.

During the best part of three days and nights the fire raged, until for lack of fuel the flames finally died out; and Norfolk, the principal town of Virginia, was reduced to a mass of charred and smoking ruins. Only twelve isolated houses escaped destruction.

One seaman, aboard the *Otter*, gloried in the event and his letter, when it reached home was printed in two of London's leading newspapers. He said:

"I have the pleasure to assure you that this rebel town of Norfolk is in ashes. It is glorious to see the blaze of the town and shipping. I exult in the carnage of these rebels. The signal was given from the *Liverpool*, and in an instant the place was in flames. We are now proceeding on this business, and will burn every port on the sea shore."

Meanwhile, news of Governor Dunmore's progressively hostile activities had been carried north and reached Thomas Jefferson. For a long time he had been worried lest "all the plantations on our river sides" be laid in waste. Here was a situation, he felt, typical of the misrule of the King of Great Britain. Writing to a friend in Virginia, Jefferson said:

"It is an immense misfortune, to the whole empire to have a King of such a disposition at such a time. We are told, and everything proves it true, that he is the bitterest enemy we have."

As the end of December approached, Thomas Jefferson grew increasingly anxious to return to Monticello. For long weeks at a stretch he had had no word from his family and he found the suspense "too terrible to be endured."

So, three days after Christmas, he secured a leave of absence from Congress and set out for Virginia.

Before Jefferson reached home he learned the fate of Norfolk.

11

The Mysterious Pamphlet

There was no ringing of joy bells when the year 1776 began.

Americans of today cannot even say the words *seventeen seventy-six* without conjuring up a picture of Liberty victorious—a vision of waving flags and cheering multitudes, all triumphantly celebrating the birth of a free and independent nation.

But New Year's Day, 1776, meant nothing like that to Americans then alive. To some of them it was the most dismal, ominous day they had ever known. Virginia's most important town was a roaring whirlwind of flames. But far more terrible than the fire itself was the fact that it was no accident. The destruction of Norfolk, like that of Falmouth, had actually been ordered and carried out in the name of His Majesty, George III.

And there was no knowing where the next fire would be lighted. Royal government had flung out a threat: "Let the rebellious Americans do as they are told or still more of their towns will go up in smoke."

When the news of Norfolk in ashes penetrated as far north as army headquarters in Cambridge, the indignant

Commander in chief expressed his reaction in a letter. George Washington wrote:

"A few more such flaming arguments as were exhibited at Falmouth and Norfolk, added to the sound doctrine and unanswerable reasoning contained in the pamphlet, *Common Sense*, will not leave numbers at a loss to decide upon the propriety of separation."

"Numbers at a loss to decide" whether it was right or wrong to separate from Great Britain—naturally there were many who were "at a loss to decide." From their cradles these good folk had been taught that loyalty to England and the king was a virtue. On the other hand, the *Virginia Gazette* was scornful of such loyalty and openly deplored "that childish fondness for Britain, and that foolish, tame dependence on her."

It was all very confusing. But now, just a week after the burning of Norfolk, at a time when it was most needed, there appeared a mysterious pamphlet that set forth with "unanswering reasoning" just why it was right and honorable to disown King George and all his works, and why America must claim her freedom and break away from the rule of any king.

The pamphlet had been put on sale in Philadelphia on the eighth of January, but the author's name was a secret. No one seemed to know who had written it, and there was much lively questioning and guessing:

"Who wrote it? Most likely it was John Adams."

"No. They say it's the work of our Doctor Franklin."

"Well, I've heard that it was written by Samuel Adams."

All guesses were wide of the mark. At the time of publication only a handful of people in Philadelphia actually knew the name of the author. Anyway, who wrote it was a minor matter; the booklet was selling by the thousand. Everybody was reading it, talking about it, and often quarreling over it.

To the Tories, the pamphlet was the last word in treason. To the patriot, it gave clarifying reasons to back his convictions. Calm arguments addressed to reason were interspersed with fiery appeals to emotion, in terms somewhat bombastic perhaps, but all the same, very effective.

The pamphlet pointed out the disastrous results of yielding to tyranny, and at the same time roused the will to overcome it.

"O ye that love mankind!" cried the pamphlet. "Ye that dare oppose not only the tyranny, but the tyrant, stand forth! Every spot of the old world is overrun with oppression. Freedom hath been hunted round the globe. Asia and Africa have long expelled her. Europe regards her like a stranger, and England hath given her warning to depart. O! receive the fugitive, and prepare in time an asylum for mankind."

This pamphlet was called *Common Sense*.

John Adams happened to be at home in Braintree when it first appeared in the shops, and did not see a copy until he reached New York on his way back to resume his duties in Congress.

Probably he picked it up with more than ordinary interest, flipping over pages and sampling paragraphs here and there, curious to see what the booklet had to offer, for he knew that he was thought to be its author.

On the whole, Mr. Adams was pleased with what he found, and felt that Abigail would like to see the much-talked-of pamphlet, so he sent her a copy and with it a letter.

"It has been very generally propagated through the continent that I wrote this pamphlet," he told his wife. "But although I could not have written anything in so manly and striking a style, I flatter myself I should have made a more respectable figure as an architect, if I had undertaken such a work."

John Adams's deepest interest was indeed that of the architect, who designs and builds up rather than that of the wrecker, who tears down. A sound, dependable form of government for this new country was what he would work for; whereas the man who wrote *Common Sense* was by nature a born leader of rebellion. His motto was, "Where Liberty is *not*, there is my country." His strength lay in fighting unjust conditions.

Shortly, the secret of the pamphlet's authorship was out. It became generally known that the man who wrote *Common Sense* was Thomas Paine, a forty-six-year old Englishman who had come to America only two years earlier.

Tom Paine had not been born on Easy Street and at no time had life been overkind to him. From personal experience he knew the difficulties of the common man under the reign of a despotic government.

In his youth Tom had been trained as a maker of ladies' stays—stays of all things! Those heavily steeled contraptions of the day were designed to keep the human body imprisoned strictly within certain limited space and artificial form. In their lowly sphere, stays were a form of physical tyranny, and Tom Paine had no love for arbitrary restriction of any sort.

THOMAS · PAINE

He soon broke away from stay-making and restlessly drifted from one job to another, seeking some work more to his liking. After a time he secured a government position. But the pay was low. Tom got into debt, neglected his work and was dismissed.

Then came a period of odd jobs, during which he even tried his hand at writing, but not for long. After a time he returned to his old government position in the excise service, but the salary was no better than it had been the first time. So the true spirit of Tom Paine, fighter against injustice, now rose to action. He and his fellow workers banded together and demanded higher wages from government.

Tom acted as spokesman. But with results quite the opposite of his intention. Instead of higher wages for everybody, Tom received his walking papers and the label of "agitator."

Presently the resentful Englishman took ship for America, and landed in Philadelphia at a time when the Colonists were fast becoming ripe for the kind of talent so richly possessed by this rebel against despotism.

That was in 1774, when one by one the thirteen Colonies were beginning to question their relation to a mother country that demanded implicit obedience, yet was most grievously lacking in all the gentler qualities of motherhood.

In certain of the taverns along Philadelphia's water front, Tom heard open criticism of the King himself. Such daring delighted him. In America he had also found work much to his liking. All his life Tom had wanted to be a scrivener, and now he was writing for the new *Penn-*

sylvania Magazine. He wrote a little, tutored a little and talked much.

He did not, however, fall to and write his famous pamphlet out of hand and of his own initiative. Indeed, the idea of writing it seems not to have originated with him at all, but was urged upon him by Dr. Benjamin Rush, a member of Congress.

In his diary Doctor Rush says:

"I called upon Mr. Paine & suggested to him the propriety of preparing our citizens for perpetual separation of this country from G.B. [Great Britain] by means of a work of such length as would obviate all objections to it. He seized the idea with avidity & immediately began his famous pamphlet in favor of the measure. He read the sheets to me at my house as he composed them."

Here was Tom Paine's supreme opportunity and he made good. His pamphlet *Common Sense* struck at the long-cherished myth of the "divine right of kings."

Two years earlier (1774) Jefferson, in his *Summary View of the Rights of British America*, said:

"Let those flatter, who fear: it is not an American art . . . those who are asserting the rights of human nature . . . know, and will, therefore, say, that Kings are the servants, not the proprietors of the people."

Both men were denying the divine right of kings. But in 1774, comparatively few people were ready to be convinced, even if the *Summary View* had been as largely circulated in America as was Paine's *Common Sense*—which it was not. And besides, Paine's style was better understood by the mass of the citizens. On that account he was invaluable.

"Government by Kings," wrote Paine, "was the most preposterous invention the Devil ever set on foot for the promotion of idolatry."

When Paine had completed his pamphlet, Doctor Rush advised him to show it to Doctor Franklin to find out what he thought of it. Then the question of a title came up. Paine thought of calling it *Plain Truth*, says Doctor Rush, but the Doctor had a better idea. He suggested *Common Sense*. And under that name the famous pamphlet took its place in history.

Common Sense proved to be the right word, spoken at the right moment, by the right man—all too rare a combination of circumstances.

How now about that much talked of *Open Door of Reconciliation* between the Colonies and British Government? More and ever increasingly more people had begun to doubt that the door could still be open at all—even so much as a tiny crack. *Common Sense* pointed out that no good would ever come through that door even if it were open. Tom Paine's pamphlet made converts by scores. The printers worked overtime, but still they couldn't keep up with the demand.

Common Sense was a best seller.

For the public in general, *independence* was no longer a word that could be hushed out of existence. Independence must be looked at, and examined—indeed, it was up to everybody to think and talk about it.

One thing at least had become clear enough—thirteen (or thirteen hundred) little Colonies, each one standing alone, fighting alone, could never hope to gain independence. All thirteen must stand together as one. There must be a union of Colonies.

A visible symbol of this idea—the Colonies bound in union—now waved bravely in the form of a flag.

Prior to 1776, if a Colony wanted a flag other than the British flag, she invented an individual flag of her own. Massachusetts, for instance, had a white flag with a pine tree in the center and above that the motto: "An Appeal To Heaven"; while South Carolina's flag was yellow, with a rattlesnake and the warning: "Don't Tread On Me."

On January 2, 1776, the first "union" flag was unfurled, with fitting ceremonies, at Washington's headquarters.

To the eyes of the watching soldiers, the new flag seemed very different from any flag they had ever seen. There were thirteen stripes, seven red and six white—a stripe for each of the thirteen Colonies. The designer had let his inventiveness have free play with the stripes; but then in one corner of the new flag he put the British jack —the crosses of St. George and St. Andrews. So the brand new flag was not yet wholly American after all—it was a compromise, and like the hesitant people of the Colonies, it was still of two minds.

Three-quarters of the Americans were now leaning toward independence. Well, let those citizens claim the red and white stripes which made up three-quarters of the new flag. And let those who still put loyalty to a king above the welfare of their country, rest their eyes on the corner of the flag bearing the emblem of the British Empire.

So now the new Union Flag, as it was called, was hoisted in Cambridge to the accompaniment of thirteen booming cannon.

There are some curiously dramatic coincidences in history, and here is one example. It so happened that the first printed copies of the King's speech declaring the Americans to be traitors and rebels, reached the camp in Cambridge that selfsame day. But the "rebels," instead of receiving the royal word with awe and terror, kindled a bonfire with the King's proclamation.

In Congress, however, the royal document stirred up a quandary. The die-hard conservatives took alarm, for undoubtedly the spirit of rebellion was spreading and here was evidence that the King knew it. Might it not be wise, they asked, to address another message to His Majesty, a message reassuring him concerning the allegiance of the majority of his American subjects—provided of course, said subjects were granted certain freedoms?

To be sure, the King had not deigned to answer the last —the Olive Branch—petition. And suppose the Colonists as a whole were *not* loyal, but were on the point of refusing allegiance—suppose they were bent on becoming an independent nation—what then?

For a little while the matter was debated, then very quietly it was pigeon-holed. And Congress, as a body, continued to sit teetering on the fence—not quite ready to get down on either side.

General Washington, however, knew his own mind and expressed his opinion on the subject with refreshing directness. He wrote:

"If every man was of my mind, the ministers of Great Britain should know, in few words, upon what issue the cause should be put. . . . I would tell them, that we have borne much, that we had long and ardently sought for reconciliation upon honorable terms, that it has been denied us . . . that we had done every thing which could be expected from the best of subjects, that the spirit of freedom beat too high in us to submit to slavery, and that, if nothing else could satisfy a tyrant and his diabolical ministry, we were determined to shake off all connections with a state so unjust and unnatural. This I would tell them, not under covert, but in words as clear as the sun in its meridian brightness."

Certainly the King knew that something all out of tune with his own ideas was steadily growing up in America. He had known it a long time.

What was this thing? He called it rebellion, but Americans called it freedom. According to the King's point of view, if America's desire for freedom was going to interfere with his (the King's) desire for total obedience to his will, then freedom was a bad thing, it must be crushed before it grew too strong. Later, George III was to find that the same troublesome desire for freedom existed in England and would put a curb on his will to rule. But in the meantime, the King and his ministry, not at all understanding how America would react, had been busy as termites destroying whatever fundamental arguments might have supported their own case.

If their sole aim had been to force the Americans to declare independence, they could hardly have made a better job of it. For, on December 22, 1775, by an Act of Parliament, the American Colonies were officially removed from *the protection of the Crown*.

In other words, the Colonies were now to be treated as enemies.

When, toward the end of February, news of this latest move on the part of royal government reached Philadelphia, John Adams seized his pen and wrote with gusto:

"The recent Act throws thirteen Colonies out of Royal Protection, levels all Distinctions and makes us independent in Spite of all our Supplications and Entreaties. It may be very fortunate that the Act of Independency should come from the British Parliament, rather than the American Congress: But it is very odd that the Americans should hesitate at accepting such a Gift from them."

But it was not as simple as all that. John Adams knew full well that the "gift" of independence must be paid for with war. In 1776, as in our own day, the price of freedom was "blood, sweat and tears."

So behind locked doors, in secret committees, patriot members of Congress worked to make ready for a long hard war. Plans were laid for getting war supplies from France. The Colonies would need far more powder than they could possibly produce at home; and without the aid of France, America could not hold out long against powerful Great Britain.

An alliance with France was necessary; yet not a thing could be done about that as long as the American Colonies "belonged" to Britain. But let America declare herself a free country and the way would be open for negotiations with France.

With this in mind, John Adams now began to double his efforts to convince his fellow members in Congress, of the need for absolute independence. He found it hard going, for the conservatives were stubborn.

"Independency," he wrote in exasperation, "is an Hobgoblin, of so frightful Mien, that it would throw a delicate Person into fits to look it in the Face."

Then, once again royal government reached a long arm across the sea and gave the Americans still another violent shove in the direction of independence.

For some months it had been rumored that King George was shopping about Europe, trying to hire foreign troops to send against the Americans. Now came word that although Catherine the Great had refused to let him have Russian soldiers, George had found an unlimited supply of fighting men in Germany. It was only a matter of how much money he was willing to spend; and George, it was well known, could afford to hire vast numbers of men to put down rebellion in America.

So it was true! The King of Great Britain would send an army of Hessians to plunder and kill until the wretched citizens of America promised unconditional submission.

Even the conservative members of Congress were—for the moment—badly shaken. Even John Dickinson sadly admitted that he saw no alternative but independence or slavery.

Yet, there were still some of those referred to in the proverb: "None so blind as those who will not see."

12

Independence Like a Torrent

It was May of 1776. May in Virginia, where that capricious rogue of a month is truly kind and passing fair—as poets like to say she is. But Thomas Jefferson must desert all the gentle beauty of Virginia's spring and travel north to Philadelphia. No matter how reluctant he might be to leave home and family, still he must go, for Thomas Jefferson had a date with History.

Not that he thought of his attendance at Congress in any such superexalted terms as that. But he did know that a black and portentous crisis threatened America, and he intended to stand with his fellow delegates in Congress to meet it head on.

Fortunately, the trip to Philadelphia no longer took him ten full days, nor would a guide be needed. He had been over the route so often by now that every fork and turn of the road was well known to him.

The seventh of May found Jefferson northward bound, and seven days later he reached Philadelphia in time to dine with friends at the City Tavern.

The City Tavern was "a most fashionable" place, advertising itself as "a genteel Tavern, elegantly lighted," with candles of course.

That night (May 14) the pendent prisms of its elegant chandeliers must have clashed and tinkled with the vibration of manly voices. Certain of the delegates had gathered in force to bombard with questions and argument the newly arrived gentleman from Virginia.

What could Mr. Jefferson tell them of affairs in the South? In the two Carolinas, for instance, were the people actually as strong for independence as the letter-writers claimed?

And what of Virginia? Only recently Sam Adams had been heard to say that he was afraid that the Southern Colonies would "get the start of Congress in declarations of independence." Certainly Congress was balking at the leap.

Concerning Virginia, Mr. Jefferson could speak with confidence. County after county had already gone on record as wanting "Continental Congress to cast off the British yoke and declare the colonies independent." One county had even added a bit of spice to its instructions by ordering the county's delegates not only "to declare for Independency," but also "to solemnly abjure any Allegiance to his Britannick Majesty and bid him a good Night forever."

"Good night" was not yet slang, but the term, in this case, carried the same modern implication of finality.

Jefferson himself, being likewise eager for news, would ask about the state of affairs in New York and Pennsylvania. A man living as far south as Virginia could not keep up with current events in the northern Colonies.

To such a question as, "Are the conservatives of New York still in the saddle?" the answer would be slow in coming.

The gentleman addressed would perhaps clear his throat, start to speak then change his mind, shrug his shoulders and finally admit that New York seemed determined to play safe. She wouldn't say yes and she wouldn't say no. Her attitude indicated her intention to let the other Colonies talk themselves hoarse on the issue of independence if they chose to do so. New York did not care to commit herself one way or the other. At the meeting of New York's Provincial Congress there had been discreet silence on the subject—independence had not been discussed at all.

How about Pennsylvania?

Well, it seemed likely that Pennsylvania might refuse to join the other Colonies, because the Tories happened for the moment to have the whip hand. They could drive the coach regardless of where the passengers wanted to go.

Such was the state of affairs when the delegates dined that night at the City Tavern. But within a short time change would come.

For example, in Pennsylvania the Tories would not long be driving the coach whither they pleased. For the time being, a powerful group of conservatives was in control—or imagined itself to be in control. But this pressure group failed to reckon with the will of the people.

One day, less than a week after Jefferson had moved into quarters on the corner of Second and Market Streets, the State House bell began to ring—not to call a session of

Congress, but to call a town meeting of the general public.

The booming voice of the great bell could be heard throughout the city and when the bell called, the citizens were expected to drop their work at once and straightway betake themselves to the large field (commonly called "the Yard") back of the State House. So presently the streets were full of people.

It was a bleak, cheerless day. And wet. Spring in the north can be as surly as November when the mood takes her. For hours the rain had been coming down in torrents, sending rivulets of water racing zigzag along the cobbled streets and cascading from steep roofs. Later the downpour had given way to a misty drizzle, cold and penetrating.

But no matter about the weather—the crowd, damp but determined, trudged toward the Yard. Umbrellas were rare in America, and besides, a man wouldn't be found dead with one of those effeminate contraptions. A man carrying an umbrella forsooth! A joke to set the whole town laughing. Who minded the rain?

When the clamor of the bell ceased to deafen you, you could hear the clumping of heavy boots, the clatter of wooden pattens and the little splashings of disturbed mud-puddles as the undaunted people made good their way to town meeting.

Thomas Jefferson must have heard and seen this dogged, bedraggled parade, and he must have meditated on its significance and its power.

The will of the people! Here was a thing to think on. This day the ordinary man was to make convincing demonstration of his will. This town meeting was no impromptu affair, born of sudden capricious anger—although anger was present. Emotion ran high, but under control, moving toward a steady purpose. There was to be an honest showdown—all cards on the table. At least that was the intention and to that end arrangements had been made. A platform for speakers stood at one side of the Yard, a moderator had been appointed, and both the patriots and the Tories would have their say.

Now the root of the trouble concerned the power of the Loyalists in the Pennsylvania House of Assembly. They had gained control and thereupon imposed on their delegates to Congress, instructions that prevented them from voting with the other Colonies for independence— if and when that issue should come to vote. And now Philadelphians at large were out in force to protest against these coercive instructions.

To the majority of the rain-soaked and vociferous crowd, the question was already settled. In fact there was no question at all. The crowd knew its own mind and proceeded to express the same without fear or favor. Any man who spoke in praise of independence was cheered mightily; while contrary-minded speakers, trying to present the case—ever so persuasively—for the King, found themselves reduced to gasping silence by an uproar of boos and catcalls. The crowd was about four thousand strong and could make considerable noise.

According to the account of one man present, "the people behaved in such a tyrannical manner that the least opposition was dangerous. Any man who dared to oppose their opinion was insulted and hushed by their interruptions and hissing."

From which report it would seem that the people were unwilling to consider both sides of the question. They refused to listen to arguments in favor of royal government. But let it be remembered that the people, having *lived* under the royal government, already knew the nature of it—a nature which no honeyed words from its advocate could camouflage. Their decision had already been reached—what they wanted was action on their decision. And they got it.

Then and there a resolution was enthusiastically passed condemning the House for the "dangerous tendency to withdraw this Province from the happy union with other colonies which we consider our glory and protection."

So it was that Pennsylvania had a small bloodless revolution all its own.

That same night John Adams took up his pen with almost breathless optimism and wrote:

"Every Post and every Day, rolls in on Us, Independence like a Torrent . . . Here are four Colonies to the Southward who are perfectly agreed now with the four to the Northward. Five in the Middle are not yet quite so ripe; but they are very near it."

Georgia, North and South Carolina and Virginia had now all been heard from and John Adams was jubilant. For the moment, this doughty New Englander seems to have been overconfident in counting his chickens, not reckoning on the stubborn resistance of certain delegates, who still clung like limpets to the idea that reconciliation, not independence, was the goal. But John must have known in his heart that there was going to be a tough fight with the stiff-necked loyalists in Congress.

Even among the patriots there was much confusion—no one was any too sure just what freedom and "independency" would mean to Americans.

One letter-writer explained it thus: "It was expected to be a form of Government that by being independt of the rich man, every man would then be able to do as he pleasd."

The writer of the above expresses to a T, man's first crude conception of freedom; namely, that freedom is liberty to do as he pleases with no restrictions whatsoever. Such freedom is like the freedom of a child playing with matches in a powder mill. Even today we are none too sure just where to place the safety zone around the figurative powder mills of dangerous liberties. In 1776, the people were in a state of bewilderment: How ought men to act when they are free?

John Adams had advanced a step further than the letter writer in his conception of independent freedom. He believed in government by the people, but he knew that if every man were given liberty to do as he pleased, there could be no form of government at all, but only anarchy. The catch was, that John could not make up his mind on that little matter of just who were "the people."

Under that heading, he asked, "would every individual of the community, old and young, male and female, as well as rich and poor" expect to have a voice in government? Quite obviously such a thing could not be, for it was plain as the nose on your face that "children, women, and men who have no property, are too dependent upon other men to have a will of their own."

Thus far Mr. Adams doubted not that he was wholly right. But alas and alack! Mrs. Adams doubted not that he was partly wrong, indeed she was passionately convinced that her husband was totally wrong on one point.

John's way of reasoning was far too narrow for the lively-minded Abigail Adams. She knew many capable women who, while their husbands were in the army, had successfully taken over the management of the farms, in addition to their usual tasks of weaving, cooking and care of the children. She wanted the women recognized. She wrote to John:

"In the new code of laws which I suppose it will be necessary for you to make, I desire you would remember the ladies and be more generous and favorable to them than your ancestors. Remember, all men would be tyrants if they could. If particular care and attention is not paid to the ladies, we are determined to foment a rebellion, and will not hold ourselves bound by any laws in which we have no voice or representation."

A woman asking for suffrage in 1776! Whoever heard the like?

Even a hint of it was enough to send a gentleman into a fit of the dithers. Mr. Adams decided to take Wife Abigail down a peg or two by ridiculing her plea. He pretended to believe that England had discovered still another way to make trouble for America. He said:

"I begin to think the ministry as deep as they are wicked. After stirring up Tories, land-jobbers, trimmers, bigots, Canadians, Indians, negroes, Hanoverians, Hessians, Russians," etc. they were now "stimulating" the women "to demand new privileges and threaten to rebel."

But Abigail was not to be distracted. She replied:

"I cannot say that I think you are very generous to the

ladies; for, whilst you are proclaiming peace and good-will to men, emancipating all nations, you insist upon retaining absolute power over wives. But you must remember that arbitrary power is like most other things which are very hard, very likely to be broken; and, notwithstanding all your wise laws and maxims, we have it in our power, not only to free ourselves, but to subdue our masters, and, without violence. . . ." (Discerning Abigail!)

Apparently the lady was allowed the last word. Delegate Adams had his hands more than full over at the State House, where committee meetings both preceded and followed the regular sessions of Congress. For now an issue very dear to the heart of John Adams had come to the fore. Congress had finally decided to advise every Colony to cast out whatever royal government still remained, and in its place formally set up a local government "under the authority of the people."

With this accomplished, a Declaration of Independence by the United Colonies should be only one short step away.

Already drastic decisions were being made in the South. Backed by the spirited instructions from county after county, the Virginia Convention was ready for action by May 15. So, with the Union Flag flying defiantly over the capitol in Williamsburg, the members adopted a resolution to be sent to Philadelphia. It was unanimously agreed

That the Delegates appointed to represent this Colony in General Congress be instructed to propose to that respectable body to declare the United Colonies free and independent States, absolved from all allegiance to, or dependence upon, the Crown or

Parliament of Great Britain; and that they give the assent of this Colony to such declaration. . . .

With this paper in his saddlebag, a horseman set out immediately for Philadelphia; and presently the highly explosive document was flung into the midst of Congress. But when the breathless horseman delivered it, Congress received it with unruffled calm.

At the moment the gentlemen were deep in military plans and could not be distracted from their labors even by a definite and formal resolution for independence. The paper must wait its turn.

The delay was hard on the New England delegates. Sam Adams wrote to a fellow patriot in Boston:

"You know my Temper. Perhaps I may be too impatient . . . However, tomorrow a Motion will be made, and a Question I hope decided, the most important that was ever agitated in America."

At last—at very long weary last—Congress would squarely face the supreme question: To separate or not to separate from the mother country? No more side-stepping. No more pussyfooting. The question would now be answered YES or NO. So hoped the out-and-out patriots.

We may picture that fateful occasion. Congress of 1776 was a colorful assemblage. At that period a man's clothes could be rich in color and ornament without detriment to his dignity. Here, on the seventh day of June, this group of gentlemen clad in knee breeches, ruffled shirts, coats and waistcoats of ornate design—these gentlemen in powdered and becurled wigs were holding in their hands a crucial issue in the history of mankind. For the moment, they held in suspension a new and untried force —the mighty power of independent freedom.

Perhaps freedom would wreck America like a gigantic earthquake. Perhaps it could mold a new form of government nearer to the hopes and desires of mankind than ever the world had known. Which way? Which way would freedom work?

The loyalists thought earthquake. The patriots thought Utopia.

These men had power to reach into the far future and lay the very foundation for our present way of life—*ours* —yours and mine. Some of these men fully realized that they were doing just that.

Tension must have risen to the snapping point when Richard Henry Lee, delegate from Virginia, rose to offer the famous resolution beginning:

"Resolved, that these united Colonies are, and of a right ought to be, free and independent States—"

Nothing could be more forthright. John Adams devoutly seconded Lee's motion like a grand amen.

But if John and Samuel Adams thought they saw the gates of Utopia swing wide open on the instant, they must look again. Perhaps Thomas Jefferson, who spoke so little and thought so much, had been warned of coming opposition by the prim mouths and frowning brows of certain stubborn gentlemen, who intended to put up a stiff fight.

That day (Friday, June 7) there was no debate. The conservatives were at their old game of playing for time, postponing decision in the vain hope that the whole subject would melt, thaw and dissolve.

Saturday. The patriots, determined to bring matters to

a head, forced their opponents into a debate which raged until seven o'clock at night. The conservatives pleaded for caution: "Even if America did want independence. why say so out loud? Why *declare* independence? Far better to work quietly and say nothing!" but the courageous New Englanders stuck to their point.

Sunday. John Adams, taking advantage of a free day, wrote letters. To one friend he wrote: "Objects of the most stupendous magnitude, and measures in which the lives of millions yet unborn are intimately interested [an understatement, Mr. Adams, we are more than interested!] are now before us. We are in the very midst of a revolution, the most complete, unexpected, and remarkable, of any in the history of nations."

Monday. At ten o'clock Congress again "considered" Mr. Lee's motion. The "sensible part of the House," says Mr. Rutledge (conservative, of course) continued to "oppose the motion." Mr. Rutledge himself was determined "that it [the decision on the measure] should be postponed for 3 Weeks or Months."

To this John Adams and his group replied that it would be vain to wait either weeks or months for perfect unanimity, since it was impossible that all men should ever become of one sentiment on any question.

Finally, both sides agreed to postpone decision to July 1.

But the patriots would let no grass grow under their feet. A committee was promptly appointed to draft a Declaration of Independence—"in case the Congress agrees thereto." In which case the document would be ready and no time lost.

Five outstanding men were chosen: John Adams, the

"Atlas of Independence," forty-one years old; Benjamin Franklin, seventy years old and as everyone agreed, an extremely wise gentleman; Thomas Jefferson, thirty-three years old, a man whose "happy talent for composition" was conceded by all; Roger Sherman, aged fifty-five and known as "a solid, sensible man"; and finally, young Robert R. Livingston who was only twenty-nine, but an active member of the conservative group. These were the members appointed to draft the Declaration.

The goddess of Liberty was growing apace. To watch her development was like watching some mysterious process of evolution. First in order of its importance came the desire for freedom: the *will* to be free. Not all nations have the will to be free.

With America's will for freedom came *ideas* and thoughts concerning what freedom is and why men have the right to demand it. And now, to make these things clearly understood, it was necessary to express them in words.

The Declaration of Independence is the spirit of America made manifest—the spirit of freedom set to words.

13

When in the Course of Human Events

From the first there seems to have been only one man who raised some question as to which one of the committee of five should draft the Declaration of Independence. That man was Thomas Jefferson.

Years later, John Adams gave a detailed account of the conversation which (according to him) took place between Jefferson and himself when the subject was under discussion. The conversation ran as follows:

"Jefferson proposed to me to make the draft. I said, I will not!

" 'You should do it.'

"Oh! no.

" 'Why will you not? You ought to do it.'

"I will not.

" 'Why?'

"Reasons enough.

" 'What can be your reasons?'

"Reason first—You are a Virginian, and a Virginian ought to appear at the head of this business. Reason second

—I am obnoxious, suspected, and unpopular. You are very much otherwise. Reason third—You can write ten times better than I can.

" 'Well, if you are decided, I will do as well as I can.' "

Mr. Adams's arguments prevailed; Jefferson went to his lodgings and set about his appointed task.

At this time Jefferson was living in a house which stood on the corner of Market and Second Streets, a pleasant house, new and airy. It was three stories high and made of brick, red and black laid alternately. Probably the owner himself had had a hand in its building for he was a bricklayer by trade. All unguessed by him, his name Graff would be remembered by history because it was in his brick house that the Declaration of Independence was written.

Another artisan who touched the fringe of fame by virture of that same document, was Ben Randolph, Philadelphia cabinet maker. He it was who built the desk at which Jefferson sat while he wrote. The desk was a most ingenious bit of furniture, designed by Jefferson himself. It was portable and, when folded up, was no bigger than a large book, yet there was room for a convenient drawer to hold paper and quills.

Jefferson had rented the entire second floor of Graff's house, which gave him a parlor with many windows, as well as a bedroom. Here then, in the parlor, at his little desk, Thomas Jefferson sat him down to write.

He used no books of reference, nor needed any. For years he had made an intensive study of the problem of the basic rights of mankind in general; and in particular, the rights (and wrongs) in the relationship between a colony and its mother country.

Thomas Jefferson sought for truth. He was not seeking to invent some original and heretofore unimagined solution to the problems of America, any more than a man adding up a column of figures seeks to invent an original sum total. No man has ever *invented* a truth, but once in a while he perceives it. Thomas Jefferson not only saw the truth and justice of America's desire for independent freedom, he also had the power to express it in words: words so forthright and crystal clear that all the world might see and understand—if it would.

Jefferson headed the paper:

A Declaration by the Representatives of the UNITED STATES OF AMERICA in General Congress assembled.*

Then came the now-familiar words:

"When in the course of human events—"

On and on raced the quill, sometimes pausing while Jefferson reconsidered—going back to reread a sentence, then drawing a line through it and writing above, words which better expressed his idea.

"We hold these truths to be sacred and undeniable that all men are created equal—"

The phrase *sacred and undeniable* was not allowed to stand. It was scratched out and above was written the single, sharper word, *self-evident*.

Driving straight to the heart of the matter, moved the inspired pen:

* The complete text of the Declaration of Independence in final form will be found at the close of Chapter 21.

"That all men are created equal; that they are endowed by their Creator with certain inalienable rights; that among these are life, liberty & the pursuit of happiness—"

If Congress accepted the Declaration it would become America's official statement, therefore it must present America's case to the world at large—give just and righteous reasons for breaking away from Great Britain. Jefferson continued:

"The history of the present majesty is a history of repeated injuries and usurpations . . . all having in direct object the establishment of an absolute tyranny over these states, to prove this let facts be submitted to a candid world."

The facts to be submitted—"the injuries and usurpations"—were much the same as those listed in Jefferson's earlier paper, *The Summary Rights of British America*. However, there were so many grievances that it would be necessary to limit the list, to exclude such examples as the Stamp Act and the Boston Port Bill, and instead, to direct attention to the King's interference with America's right to make laws for herself.

Jefferson wrote:

"He [the King] has dissolved representative houses repeatedly & continually for opposing with manly firmness his invasions on the rights of the people. . . .

"He has kept among us in times of peace standing armies and ships of war without the consent of our legislatures. . . .

"He has plundered our seas, ravaged our coasts, burnt our towns & destroyed the lives of our people.

"He is at this time transporting large armies of foreign mercenaries to compleat the works of death, desolation & tyranny already begun with circumstances of cruelty & perfidy unworthy the head of a civilized nation."

The question of slavery had long troubled Jefferson. His ideas for the emancipation of Negroes were not shared by his fellow Virginians; nevertheless, he believed that "nothing is more certainly written in the book of fate, than that these people are to be free."

That Jefferson should write into this first draft of the Declaration, "the section concerning negro slavery" was a foregone conclusion. But you will not find it in the final document, for it was not allowed to stand. Even while he wrote, Jefferson must have known that there was little chance of its winning the approval of Congress. Yet he must record his own belief that, in the matter of slavery, the King had "waged cruel war against human nature itself. . . ."

"Determined to keep open market where MEN should be bought & sold, he has prostituted his negative for suppressing every legislative attempt to prohibit or to restrain this execrable commerce."

Mindful of the many petitions addressed to the King, Jefferson wrote:

"In every stage of these oppressions we have petitioned for redress in the most humble terms: our repeated petitions have been answered by repeated injuries."

Page after page was filled with Jefferson's clear script. Then finally came the closing words:

"And for the support of this declaration we mutually pledge to each other, our lives, our fortunes & our sacred honor."

Jefferson does not say how much time he spent on this first draft; but John Adams believed that it took him only "a day or two." In any case, as soon as Jefferson had completed the draft to his own satisfaction, he sought out John Adams and asked for his opinion.

Says Adams: "We conned the paper over, I was delighted with its high tone and the flights of oratory with which it abounded."

Mr. Adams was also delighted with "the section concerning negro slavery, which," says Adams "though I knew his Southern brethren would never suffer to pass in Congress, I certainly never would oppose."

John Adams found little to criticize—he suggested only a minor change or two in the wording. For instance, instead of *majesty*, he would use the phrase *King of Great Britain.*

Jefferson agreed, and later the words, "King of Great Britain" were interlined on the draft in Adams's handwriting.

Since he valued the opinions of John Adams and Benjamin Franklin above all others, Jefferson next called on Doctor Franklin. The old gentleman also approved the draft, but felt that a little different wording here or there might add to its force.

Take the phrase *answered by repeated injury*, for example. With the addition of the single word *only*—Franklin pointed out—the sentence would gain strength: "answered *only* by repeated injury."

Fortunately for the student of today, Jefferson's original draft, with the revisions—two added in the handwriting of Adams, and five by Franklin—is in the safekeeping of the Library of Congress.

Jefferson now set himself to writing a fair copy to be submitted by the committee to Congress. Congress, he had been informed, was impatient to see the document. Undoubtedly some of the members were more impatient to see it than were others.

On the twenty-eighth of June, a Friday, Jefferson's draft was formally presented to the House and then read, but without comment.

It was "ordered to lie on the table," says Jefferson briefly.

Apparently Congress, having heard for the first time one of the most remarkable documents ever written, listened in tight-lipped silence: the kind of silence you can cut with a knife, the quietude that precedes a storm. Certainly the storm was coming. It was due to break on Monday, July 1.

A July day can be ferociously hot in Philadelphia and Monday was such a day. The sun beat with unmerciful glare on brick houses and cobbled streets; and the long, unkempt grass in the State House Yard was seared to well-dried hay. The very dogs in the vicinity sought shelter from the sun and lolled panting in what little protection might be found in the shadow of the building, there being never a tree in the Yard to shade them.

John Adams had been up since an early hour, writing letters. Referring to the Declaration, he wrote:

"This day or tomorrow is to determine its fate. May Heaven prosper the new-born republic, and make it more glorious than any former republics have been!"

Mr. Adams faced the day with confidence, although no one knew better than he what a stiff fight lay ahead, and that he himself would probably have to bear the brunt of it.

The fight would center on Lee's "resolution respecting independency." Meanwhile the Declaration of Independence must lie unheeded on the table. Until (or unless) Lee's resolution was accepted by Congress, there was no point in discussing the *manner* of declaring independence. Possibly Jefferson's over-frank paper could be torn up and flung to the winds—the conservatives devoutly hoped as much.

The negative side fought valiantly.

Up rose the tall and somber Mr. Dickinson, leader of the conservatives of Pennsylvania. He was earnest and sincere in his conviction that breaking away from the mother country was something akin to suicide for the Colonies. Mr. Dickinson most ably (though unintentionally) demonstrated the fact that a man may be earnest and sincere and totally wrong—all at the same time.

The earnest gentleman could offer nothing new in support of his cause. He talked a weary while, "repeating," says John Adams, "all that had, from time to time, been

147

said in Congress by himself and others." Which must have been a considerable amount.

At last Mr. Dickinson talked himself out—ran down like a clock and was silent. He resumed his seat; now it was up to the patriots.

Naturally, everyone expected a certain hot-headed New Englander to spring to it with the speed and fire of lightning. Instead of that the meeting went dead—flat as a flounder. Here and there heads were turned toward Delegate John Adams. Surely he would take up the challenge.

But Mr. Adams continued to sit quietly, making no move to take the floor.

The faces of the men who believed in a free America, now began to register consternation. Questioning eyebrows were raised. Why was Mr. Adams so reluctant to speak?

Several of the delegates began to prod him. Said one, "You have had the subject at heart longer than any of us, you must recapitulate the arguments."

Mr. Adams has recorded his reason for thus holding back. He would have the cause defended by "some one less obnoxious than myself, who had been all along for a Year before, and still was represented and believed to be the Author of all the Mischief."

But one can't help suspecting the experienced Mr. Adams of being fully aware of the drama of the situation. The period of silence, the seeming reluctance, were bound to gain breathless attention for his opening words.

Presently he rose and began to speak:

"This is the first time in my life," he said, "that I seriously wish for the genius and eloquence of the celebrated orators of Athens and Rome, for I am sure that none of them ever had before him a question of more importance to his country and to the world. . . ."

But even lacking the eloquence of the ancient orators, Mr. Adams did well. Later, one of the delegates was to declare enthusiastically: "The Man to whom the country is most indebted for the great measure of Independence is Mr. John Adams of Boston. I call him the Atlas of independence. He it was who sustained the debate and . . . by force of his reasonings, demonstrated not only the justice but the expediency of the measure!"

John Adams had not attempted to make his points by painting rosy pictures of any Utopian land of the free. He saw clearly enough the pitfalls which lay ahead.

"If you imagine that I expect the Declaration will ward off calamities from this country," he told his fellow delegates, "you are much mistaken. A bloody conflict we are destined to endure—this has been my opinion from the beginning . . . But Freedom is a counter-balance for poverty, discord, and war, and more."

By four o'clock that afternoon the glaring sun was curtained by black clouds that rolled ponderously above the city. The Assembly Chamber grew dark. Then came sharp lightning, crash of thunder and wind-driven rain hissing against the windows of the State House. A "thundergust" in that part of our country is as magnificent a battle of the elements as one could wish to see. And while the thunderstorm raged outside, the storm of controversy raged inside the House with no less violence. Congress kept at it hour after hour, without rest and without food.

When a flash of lightning cut through the gloom of that room, it must have lit with unearthly brilliance the white faces of the men who were deciding the fate of a nation.

All this time Thomas Jefferson had been industriously taking notes—keeping track of exactly what was taking place. He says:

"It was now evening, the members exhausted by a debate of nine hours, during which all the powers of the soul had been distended with the magnitude of the object—without refreshment, without pause—and the delegates of South Carolina desired that the final decision might be put off to the next morning that they might still weigh in their own minds their ultimate vote." Their motion was carried.

By nine o'clock the sky was clear. Moonlight flooded the streets, greatly aiding the tired delegates in finding their way home, or to some neighboring tavern.

There was one delegate, however, who gave no thought to food or rest. Thomas McKean was extremely disturbed by the knowledge that while he, delegate from Delaware, would vote for independence, his fellow delegate from the same Colony would vote against it, thus nullifying Delaware's vote. But there was one solution, if only there was time to carry it out. He must get word to Caesar Rodney—the third delegate of the Colony, but absent at the moment, who would, Mr. McKean knew, vote in the affirmative.

Unfortunately Mr. Rodney was in Dover—the best part of a hundred miles to the south. And since Lee's resolution might be put to vote early the next day, there seemed little chance of Rodney's reaching Philadelphia in time to cast his vote for independence.

But McKean was willing to gamble on it—even to the extent of paying the express rider out of his own pocket. Presently he did succeed in locating a rider. So, while the night was still fairly young, the route to Dover rang with the beat of hoofs.

14

Three Critical Days

Tuesday, *July 2, 1776.* Heavy gray clouds blanketed the sky, and the City of Brotherly Love was enjoying a brief respite from yesterday's heat.

Old Doctor Franklin welcomed the drop in temperature, but the dampness tended to increase the pain in his poor foot. For several weeks past he had been suffering from a severe attack of gout, and even the bare thought of changing from soft house slippers to street shoes was enough to make him cringe. Nevertheless, he must venture out today. He had already missed so many sessions of Congress that he'd rather lost track of its doings. As he had recently written to General Washington, he knew "little of what has pass'd there except that a Declaration of Independence is preparing."

But if he had cared to admit it, the old gentleman knew considerable about the draft for the document, for he had already been over the paper with Thomas Jefferson and approved it. And now he intended to be on hand in the Assembly Chamber to cast his vote for independence— even if it killed him to get there!

The patriots agreed that it was not enough to have the

measure passed by majority vote; they wanted the vote to be unanimous. Yet even the most optimistic among them must have wondered if such a thing was within the bounds of possibility, what with Delaware's vote divided, and New York's delegates still without instructions from the Colony's Provincial Assembly, and South Carolina most uncertain. Indeed, every member of Congress, who had passed through that devastating battle of debate on Monday, must have wakened on Tuesday to find himself in a very torment of anxiety and suspense.

In the case of Delegate McKean, two questions must surely have haunted his dreams: Could the express rider locate Rodney? And even if he did, could Rodney manage to reach Philadelphia before the final vote on independence was cast?

McKean had not been able to give the messenger explicit directions—there was no telling exactly where Caesar Rodney could be found. Some time earlier, he had been excused from Congress because of trouble threatening on the lower Delaware—certain Tories were getting out of hand and Rodney had ridden down to help straighten out the matter.

The story of Rodney's long hard ride has been told over and again. And, as so often happens in the case of some particularly dramatic incident in history, the teller of the tale cannot resist touching it up a bit, for the sake of making it appear still more sensational. Then, next time the story is retold, the sensational version is relied upon as fact and again embellished by a few more dramatic flourishes. In the instance of Rodney's ride, this procedure has been repeated so often that Rodney himself would not recognize his own adventure.

For example, we may read of Caesar Rodney breathlessly galloping into Philadelphia at the eleventh hour, flinging himself from his spent horse, dashing his way into the State House, across the Assembly Chamber, and, hand trembling with haste, adding his signature to the Declaration of Independence—the last signature at the last second before dead line!—thus saving the day and the whole future of America!

Or again, with no hint that the author of the tale is drawing on his own imagination, we read that the door of the State House "burst open" to admit a man "with face as pale as ashes" who "rushed upon the floor" while the members, taken by surprise, "clapped their hands to their sword hilts," while others (we are told) shielded their faces with their arms as if to protect themselves against attack.

Yet what actually happened is a matter of record. Thomas McKean himself set it down in black and white. He wrote:

"I sent an express (at my private expense) for Caesar Rodney, the member for Delaware, whom I met at the State house door in his boots and spurs, as the members were assembling."

But despite that calm statement, there is still plenty of good drama left in the story of Rodney's famous ride.

It seems that he was already on his way to Philadelphia when he came upon the messenger bearing the letter from McKean. But many long miles still lay before him, and if he was to reach Philadelphia by Tuesday morning, in time to cast his vote for Lee's resolution (not *sign* the Declaration) Rodney knew that he must ride as fast as a horse could carry him. There could be no stopping for food or rest—and certainly no time in which to take shelter from a storm.

That night the skies opened and let loose a deluge of rain. Except for blinding flashes of lightning, the road was black as your hat. Wind whipped at the rider's surtout and snatched at his three-cornered hat, and the crashes of thunder were enough to madden even a tired horse.

Rodney's own account of that grueling ride is all too brief, but he does not leave out that thunderstorm.

He rode eighty difficult miles—this man past middle age, whom John Adams called, "the oddest looking man in the world . . . so tall and thin" and with a head "no bigger than a large apple." Yet when Rodney reached Philadelphia on Tuesday morning, he was not too exhausted to go directly to the State House.

In the Yard he found Delegate Read, and the two were deep in conversation when Thomas McKean arrived. So together the three men entered the building—Rodney still wearing his riding boots and spurs—but the members present did not clap frightened hands to sword hilt! Why on earth should they?

That same night Caesar Rodney himself summed up the day's happenings in a single sentence. He wrote: "It [independence] is determined by the thirteen United Colonies, without one decenting Colony."

Richard Henry Lee's "resolution respecting independency" had indeed been passed without one "decenting" Colony. Twelve Colonies had voted in the affirmative.

The New York delegates, without authority to vote yes, had done the next best thing—they had kept silent.

Both John Dickinson and Robert Morris, conservative Pennsylvanians, had discreetly stayed at home on this second day of July, thus permitting their Colony's vote to be a resounding yes. South Carolina too, had finally decided to stand with her sister Colonies so that the vote could be unanimous.

Late Tuesday afternoon (July 2) the weather again became breathlessly hot, but the gentlemen of Congress were not to be deterred by the rising mercury. Immediately following the acceptance of Lee's resolution, the committee for drafting the Declaration had presented Jefferson's paper for consideration.

Consideration is scarcely the word. It would seem that almost every delegate from every one of the Colonies considered it his bounden duty to suggest some other way of writing the Declaration than the way Jefferson had written it. Suggestions for changes came thick and fast as rain drops, nor did there seem to be any end to them. At this rate, consideration of Jefferson's paper was not to take mere hours, but whole days, before agreement could be reached. And this was only the beginning!

John Adams, however, was in too high spirits to be worried either by the heat or the length of debate. He was sure that the second of July would be regarded by future generations as the turning point in American history. He wrote to Abigail:

"I am apt to believe that it [July 2] will be celebrated by succeeding generations as the great anniversary festival.

It ought to be commemorated as the day of deliverance, by solemn acts of devotion to God Almighty. It ought to be solemnized with pomp and parade, with shows, games, sports, guns, bells, bonfires, and illumination, from one end of this continent to the other, from this time forward forevermore."

Mr. Adams previsioned the celebration of the birthday of a nation, but—as he himself would live to discover—the date of that birthday would not be July 2, when Lee's resolution was adopted, but the Fourth of July—the day the Declaration of Independence was accepted.

Wednesday, July 3, 1776. The morning dawned bright and fair. A fresh wind was blowing, clearing the city of Tuesday's heat. And Congress, refreshed and eager for the fray, gave itself heart, soul and strength to the "great and solemn" debate. Not a page, not a sentence, not a word would be accepted without first going through the fiery ordeal of criticism.

Jefferson made no attempt to defend his paper, or to explain why he had seen fit to include certain phrases which were bound to cause vociferous and violent argument. Instead, he was silent. He believed it his "duty to be . . . a passive auditor of the opinions of others." To let "more impartial judges" than he could be, pass on "its merits and demerits."

Jefferson had an almost unbelievable power of self-control. He could hold his tongue even when he found the discussion most unpalatable, but he does admit to "writhing a little under the acrimonious criticism."

When Congress adjourned for the day, no conclusion

157

had been reached. As far as the curious public was concerned, there was "nothing to report." A veil of secrecy hung over what was happening at the State House.

But lack of official news never did hamper the tongues of the customers at the Coffee House. There was always plenty of backstair information—both fact and fiction—to pass across the tables of a tavern.

Thursday, July 4, 1776. A pleasant morning wind ruffled the dusty leaves of shade trees. The sunshine, although hot was cheerful. Later on in the day it would become a blinding glare, and shimmering waves of hot air would rise from the baking cobblestones of Chestnut Street.

Inside the State House, however, the delegates were at it again tooth and nail—too engrossed in hot discussion to heed the torrid temperature. Occasionally, a man might mop his damp brow with a handkerchief of fine linen, or run a finger inside the high stock that swathed his throat. But what of that? The debate over Jefferson's draft of the Declaration of Independence was all-absorbing.

Certain of the delegates objected to the accusations against the British people—thereupon many lines were deleted. Other delegates—especially those from the South— were demanding that the whole passage concerning the Negro slave trade be cut out. They argued that the question of Negro slavery was not one of the grievances which had caused the rebellion. They said it had nothing to do with America's reasons for declaring independence.

So that entire section, although particularly dear to Jefferson's heart, was stricken out.

There were certain changes which, it must be agreed,

FRANKLIN·APPROVED·THE·DRAFT·

were to the good, such as the dropping of a word or two and the substitution of a different word. For instance, *a people who mean to be free* was simplified to, *a free people*. And for the phrase, *were likely to*, was substituted *would inevitably*.

And so it went, the members weighing and testing every word, but sometimes going to such extremes in their effort to be wise, that they achieved only mutilation.

"Timothy [Pickering]," wrote the sorely tried author of the Declaration, "thinks the instrument the better for having a fourth of it expunged. He would have thought it still better had the other three fourths gone also, all but one single sentiment (the only one he approves) which recommends friendship to his dear England, whenever she is willing to be at peace with us."

During all the hours of tearing his paper to bits and rending it limb from limb—although he could "take it" and submit in silence—Jefferson must have stirred uneasily in his chair, shifting his weight, crossing and uncrossing his long legs. He was sitting next to Doctor Franklin and the old gentleman noticed that the young man was miserable under the mutilations.

The sympathic Doctor Franklin leaned toward Jefferson and spoke in a quiet voice.

"I make it a rule," said he, "whenever in my power, to avoid becoming the draughman of papers to be reviewed by a public body. I took my lesson from an incident which I will relate to you. When I was a journeyman printer, one of my companions, an apprentice Hatter, having served out his time, was about to open a shop for himself. His first concern was to have a handsome sign-board, with a proper inscription. He composed it in these words—John Thompson, *Hatter, makes* and *sells hats for ready money*—with a figure of a hat subjoined.

"The first he showed it to thought the word *Hatter*, tautologous, because followed by the words *makes hats* which showed he was a Hatter. It was struck out.

"The next observed that the word *makes* might as well be omitted, because his customers would not care who made the hats. If good and to their mind, they would buy, by whomsoever made. He struck it out.

"A third said he thought the words *for ready money* were useless as it was not the custom of the place to sell on credit. Everyone who purchased expected to pay. They were parted with, and the inscription now stood, *John Thompson sells hats*.

"'Sells hats'!" says his next friend. 'Why nobody will expect you to *give* them away. What then is the use of that word?' It was stricken out, and *hats* followed it, the rather, as there was one painted on the board.

"So his inscription was reduced ultimately to *John Thompson* with the figure of a hat subjoined."

Rest assured John Adams and his group were not taking the savage rending apart of Jefferson's work in any spirit of silent submission. Far from it.

"He [Adams] supported the Declaration of Independence with zeal and ability, fighting fearlessly for every word of it," wrote Jefferson later.

Fighting? The contending parties had begun action on Tuesday. From that time on, all day Wednesday and all day Thursday, the Assembly Chamber rang with the "clash of resounding arms." Not until the evening of July 4, did the battle of debate come to an end. Then at last the delegates arrived at a point of mutual agreement on the exact wording of the document.

And now the tired fighters settled back in their chairs to listen quietly while Benjamin Harrison, of Virginia, read aloud in its accepted form, America's Declaration of Independence.

Through the open windows drifted the usual street noises—the clatter of hoofs, the rattle of wheels, and perhaps the distant voice of the town crier. But no expectant crowd had collected in the State House Yard, waiting a dramatic announcement by the doorkeeper that the Declaration of Independence had been accepted by the House. No bulletins had been issued to the public during the course of the debate, and no proclamation of acceptance would be made—not on the Fourth of July.

Familiar as the delegates were with every line and paragraph of Jefferson's document (for despite editing, it was still the work of Jefferson)—the words, as Harrison read, took on fresh force, affecting every man present. No longer did the delegates lean back in their chairs. They had become tense and strangely keyed. Harrison himself had difficulty in keeping his voice steady—again and again he found it necessary to pause lest he betray the emotion he was struggling to control.

So, reverently, without benefit of trumpet and drum, the Declaration of Independence was solemnly adopted by "the Representatives of the United States of America in General Congress Assembled."

15

Proclaim Liberty Throughout all the Land

"The big bell will ring at noon."

The word passed from one to another until everyone knew; but the people did not wait until twelve o'clock. Well before that hour men, women and children in holiday attire were heading toward the open field behind the State House.

"Best to go early if you want to get close enough to hear —there's bound to be a most uncommon crowd of folk on hand," so said the wise ones.

Fortunately, the day was bright and gay as hope fulfilled, not a rain cloud in the blue sky. Perhaps the sun was a trifle too hot, but better that than no sunshine. For 'twould be a sad omen if joy in the first Independence Day were to be dampened by a downpour.

As it was, the celebration was four days late, for this was the eighth of July. But even if late there must be a celebration and this was the day appointed by Congress. In fact, under the circumstances, the eighth was the first possible date. The Declaration had been accepted too late on Thursday the fourth to permit plans for celebration on Saturday. Sunday, of course was out of the question. So Monday, the eighth, it must be.

All manner of plans had been made. There would be a parade, then the new Declaration would be read from a special stage in the Yard, to the assembled citizens. In the evening there would be great doings on the Common.

State House Yard, in 1776, was far different from Independence Square of today. Instead of our pleasant Square, with its stretches of green lawn, neatly laid out walks and many fine shade trees, the Yard was like a rough country field, without a single tree to its name. And the "stage" from which Colonel Nixon was to read the Declaration, was a high wooden platform with a railing, built around the circular observatory which had been erected some years earlier. The platform, in honor of today's occasion, was gaily decked with flags, and from near-by windows of the State House fluttered more flags.

By high noon the Yard was packed with thousands of spectators who stood with bated breath, while overhead the great bell in the tower above the State House boomed its message of freedom.

Always, since the day it was cast, the bell had been girdled by its proclamation of liberty, but never before had it freely, without reservation, flung that passionate proclamation to all the winds of Heaven. Now it rang out its message in full:

Proclaim Liberty Throughout all the Land unto all the Inhabitants Thereof.

Then all the bells of the city joined in chorus.

"Even the chimes chimed away," says John Adams. And while the bells were in full cry the procession appeared. The crowd in the Yard, now at high tension of excitement, was ready to cheer. First came the Committee of Safety and the Committee of Inspection accompanied by the "important" gentlemen of the city. Then came the tall, dignified Colonel Nixon, carrying one of the newly printed copies of the Declaration of Independence. The lusty open-mouthed cheering that greeted him could be seen rather than heard, for the voice of the Liberty Bell alone could outshout a roaring multitude. Nor did it cease its noisy ringing until the minute that Colonel Nixon appeared on the high platform. With him were many members of Congress and high Army officers.

Then silence. A hush to be broken only by the voice of Colonel Nixon:

A Declaration by the Representatives of the United States of America in General Congress assembled . . .

And so on to the closing words of the great document:

And for the support of this Declaration, with a firm reliance on the protection of divine Providence, we mutually pledge to each other our lives, our fortunes and our sacred honor.

The reading had come to an end. And now it was the people's turn.

Says John Adams, "three cheers rended the welkin."

But huzzas were not enough and the crowd shouted, "God bless the Free States of North America!"

Overhead the bell of Liberty again took the lead, setting pace for the lesser bells. All that day and almost all night they would ring without pause, for the celebration was far from over.

Now would come the gleeful and satisfying task of tearing down the King's coat of arms from all the public places. The royal symbols would make wonderful fuel for bonfires on the Common, where there would be special military parades and the firing of thirteen volleys—notwithstanding scarcity of powder—for the occasion warranted extravagance.

Most of the townspeople who had crowded the Yard at high noon to hear the official reading, already knew the content of the Declaration. The text had been printed in full in one or two of Saturday's newspapers, and there had been no lack of broadsides for handing about. The latter had been printed late Friday night, the printers having worked unceasingly to have them ready to be given, on Saturday, to express riders, mail coaches, and even to private travelers who might be going to assigned places without delay. Copies must reach the various Assemblies, Conventions, and so on, in order that the Declaration could be "proclaimed in each of the United States in such a Mode, as the People may be universally informed of it." General Washington himself would proclaim it at the head of the army.

So, the text of the Declaration began traveling in the form of broadsides (signed only by the type-set names of the president and secretary of Congress) and finally reached every city, town and hamlet throughout the length and breadth of the country, to be celebrated usually with bonfires and with prayers. Very often the King of Great

Britain (though not by royal intention) played a leading role in the celebrations.

For example, in Baltimore, "an effigy of our late King was carted through the Town and Committed to the flames amidst the acclamation of many hundreds—the just reward of a tyrant."

In New York, the King took a leading part as villain of the piece.

At the time of the repeal of the Stamp Act an equestrian statue of King George had been erected on Bowling Green as an expression of gratitude for the repeal of that oppressive law. The statue was life-size, composed of lead and brass, all richly gilded.

But now, July, 1776, the New Yorkers—no longer feeling the least spark of gratitude toward His Majesty—watched with delight while a band of sturdy patriots hauled the rampant metal steed down from his high pedestal and dismembered him. George too came in for rough handling. His head was removed, his nose chopped off and his wreath of laurels chipped and disfigured. Then the head was trundled off in a wheelbarrow and later "fixed on a spike" and exhibited before the tavern at Kingsbridge.

The rest of His Majesty and most of the horse ended in the melting pot, after which the remains of both king and horse became thousands of much needed bullets for the use of the "rebels."

Old records state that the tail of the horse and part of the saddle were carried away by spectators to be cherished as historic souvenirs. And from the journal of a British colonel we learn what eventually became of that royal head on the spike. The Colonel relates how he sent his men to steal the head and bury it for safekeeping. This they did so well that the pleased officer gave them a reward. Later, the Colonel had the head dug up to be carried to England "by Lady Gage to Lord Townshend in order to convince them at home of the infamous Disposition of the Ungrateful people of this distress'd Country."

Boston had no statue of the King to tear down. And no effigy was burned, only the King's Arms, and everything was very much as it should be.

Abigail Adams "went with the multitude into King Street to hear the Proclamation for Independence read and proclaimed." In a letter to John she said:

"The troops appeared under arms, and all the inhabitants assembled there . . . when Colonel Crafts read from the balcony of the State House the proclamation. Great attention was given to every word. As soon as he ended, the cry from the balcony was, 'God save our American States.' and then three cheers rent the air. The bells rang, the privateers fired, the forts and batteries, the cannon were joyful . . . After dinner, the King's Arms were taken down from the State House, and every vestige of him from every place in which it appeared, and burnt in King Street. Thus ends royal authority in this State. And all the people shall say Amen."

16

Engrossed on Parchment

Jefferson's draft of the Declaration of Independence was written on paper.

A piece of paper, reasonably good in quality, will last a long time if carefully protected. But in the case of a document intended to be time-proof (if that were possible), we revert to the ancient custom of writing on parchment.

Of course no one could foresee that the Declaration was destined to come in for some very rough handling and hairbreadth escapes from destruction; nevertheless, Congress fortunately did realize that it ought to be made as permanent as conditions permitted. Therefore, on July 19, an order was given that the Declaration of Independence be engrossed on parchment. And, in the place of the original title: "A Declaration By The Representatives Of The United States Of America In General Congress Assembled," there should be a new title: "In Congress, July 4, 1776. The Unanimous Declaration of the Thirteen United States of America."

The engrosser, poor man, probably urged to haste, was more concerned about his craftsmanship and the quality of his quill and the steadiness of his pen stroke, than about the words themselves. When the document was delivered to Congress a number of mistakes were discovered.

"United States" was written "united STATES." The word *British* was misspelled—there were two *t's*—and the word *only* was omitted, then interlined; the same being true of the syllable *en* in *Representative*.

But on the whole, the copy was considered acceptable. So, on August 2, came the formal signing of the document by all the members present at the time. Members unable to attend would sign later, at their convenience; among them would be Delegate Thornton of New Hampshire who, incidentally, was not even a member of Congress on July 4, when the Declaration was accepted.

President Hancock signed first, in a large firm hand. As the story goes, he purposely "wrote large" so that, as he remarked, "George III may read without his spectacles." Then the delegates signed their names. Some signatures were bold and written with a flourish, others were very small and neat.

There may well have been an air of uneasy tension during that period when one by one, the gentlemen stepped up to the President's table, picked up the quill, dipped it in ink and wrote the signature which might bring him to the "high gallows."

The signing of that document, as viewed from across the ocean by King George and his friends, was of course an act of high treason. Naturally, nothing would please His Majesty better than to deal to the fifty-six signers the penalty due "traitors."

In the summer of 1776, no man could know how the

war with Great Britain would end. At the moment things looked black for the Americans. American forces in Canada were retreating before victorious Britons; the Hessians had taken possession of Staten Island, and New York seemed doomed to fall. Moreover, the American army was dwindling at an alarming rate, partly because the men were not re-enlisting—they headed for home the instant their term of service expired—and partly because a scourge of smallpox was killing the soldiers by the hundreds.

And as if all this were not discouraging enough, there was a serious shortage of ammunition and guns. America faced the future alone—the alliance with France was still only a hope.

Yet, regardless of the outcome, the United States chose to wave her own flag of defiance and formally declare her independence. Americans would no longer fight for the *redress of wrongs;* from now on they would fight for the establishment of a *free and independent government*. And there is a vast difference between those two objectives.

The men who signed America's Declaration of Independence were risking their personal fortunes, their lives, the safety of their families—and the fate of a nation. Many of the delegates were wealthy men—they had inherited much land and money. Some were self-made. Very few were actually poor. But every last one of them had courage. They looked open-eyed into the future.

Shortly after the adoption of Lee's resolution, John Adams had written to his wife:

"You will think me transported with enthusiasm, but I am not. I am well aware of the toil, and blood and treasure, that it will cost us to maintain this declaration, and support and defend these States. Yet through all the gloom I can see the rays of ravishing light and glory. I can see that the end is worth more than all the means, and that posterity will triumph in that day's transaction, even although we shall rue it, which I trust in God we shall not."

No man had worked more earnestly than John Adams to bring about "that day's transaction." By September of '76, he was thoroughly tired. The humid summer heat of Philadelphia had been very wearing and he yearned for "the bracing quality" of his "native air." But there were too many knotty problems before Congress for him to leave before October. At last, on the thirteenth of that month, he was able to depart at a comfortable pace for Braintree, Massachusetts. He would be at home for the next three months.

Jefferson too had been longing for a chance to return to his home. In drafting the Declaration, he had used to the full his own great gift, and he felt that he was no longer urgently needed in Congress. In August, when the question of accepting a new term as delegate from Virginia, came up Jefferson declined, stating that he thought he "could be of more use . . . in the legislature of my state." So anxious was he to return to Virginia—every letter from Monticello had brought such disheartening reports of his wife's health—that it was only "with pain" that he remained in Philadelphia until the latter part of August when Colonel Lee, his successor, arrived—that worthy gentleman having been delayed by "the slowness of the workman that made my [Lee's] Carriage Wheels, the old being shattered & useless."

When, in due course, the text of rebellious America's Declaration had crossed the Atlantic to London and reached the King, it was received in characteristic manner. George III, in a speech, dismissed this latest move on America's part as simply more of the same—treasonable of course, but not without remedy. And he would see that the remedy was applied. His Majesty gave warning:

"If their Treason be suffered to take Root, much Mischief may grow from it to the safety of my loyal Colonies, to the Commerce of my Kingdoms, and indeed to the present System of all Europe."

In the House of Peers, however, were sturdy Englishmen who dared express their approval even when their ideas ran counter to those entertained by the Crown.

"The Ministers," declared John Wilkes, "drove the Americans into their present state on independency. This [declaration] was done with circumstances of spirit and courage to which posterity will do justice. I hope and believe, you never will conquer the free spirit of the descendents of Englishmen, exerted in an honest cause. They value the blessings of liberty."

Thus spoke in prophecy the true spirit of England.

17

The First Anniversary

New Year's Day, 1777, found the city of Philadelphia in a state of semipanic. For weeks past, a dispiriting rumor had been whispered about town: Congress was preparing to flee! The delegates had "inside" information, it was said, and if they were leaving it was a sure sign that the city was in grave danger of capture by the British.

The gentlemen of Congress vigorously denied the charge. They even went so far as to instruct General Washington to denounce the "scandalous report."

Nevertheless, all statements to the contrary, by the middle of December the members of Congress had indeed packed up and fled in confusion, some of them riding northward, others traveling south, although all of them were supposedly journeying to Baltimore.

John Adams was not in Philadelphia at this time, having gone home in October; but on the ninth of January he mounted his horse and rode forth to join his fellow delegates.

Judging from the tone of his letters, written during this journey, Mr. Adams was not in the least disturbed by the knowledge that Congress had suddenly adjourned to Baltimore. In letters to Abigail, John dwelt on the "good news" that General Washington had "gained another considerable advantage of the enemy at Stony Brook, in the Jerseys."

By the time Delegate Adams had reached New York, his letters were full of references to the severe winter weather. At Poughkeepsie he found the Hudson filled with cakes of ice—too much ice "to cross it in ferry-boats, and too little to cross it without." There was nothing for it but to ride for many miles along the bank of the river, until he and his party managed to find a place with ice sufficiently solid to enable them to ride their horses across.

"After the longest journey and through the worst roads and the worst weather that I have ever experienced," John Adams arrived in Baltimore. There he found his colleagues none too happy over the location.

As Benjamin Rush put it: "We live here in a Convent, we converse only with one another. We are precluded from all opportunities of feeling the pulse of the public upon our measures."

What seems to have impressed John most was the conspicuous lack of former delegates. "I have the mealoncholy Prospect before me," he wrote, "of a Congress continually changing, untill very few Faces remain, that I saw in the first Congress."

Samuel Adams was still a member, so too were Richard Henry Lee and Roger Sherman and a few other signers of the Declaration of Independence, but all the others, John told Abigail, "are dead, resigned, deserted or cutt up into Governors, etc. at home."

A·RUMOR·WENT·THE·ROUNDS

Barely more than two weeks after the travel-weary John Adams rode into Baltimore, Congress decided that its flight from Philadelphia had been premature, and thereupon the members packed up and returned to Philadelphia.

During the spring, Congress strove to draw up a plan of Confederation which would permit each of the thirteen States to retain complete "sovereignty, freedom and independence," and yet, at the same time, work together in harmony as *united* States. A herculean task! But at least the delegates could now consider this difficult problem with comparative peace of mind. There was no more disturbing talk of Philadelphia's being captured by the enemy.

And on the Fourth of July, the first anniversary of the birthday of the nation could be celebrated with all the pomp and circumstance a people at war could muster— which was considerable.

Troops paraded the crowded streets, past houses proudly displaying the newly adopted national flag—the Stars and Stripes—while cannon boomed.

Says the *Pennsylvania Gazette*, "Small arms, and loud huzzahs resounded from street to street through the city. A Hessian band of music [prisoners of war] heightened the festivity with some fine performances suited to the joyous occasion." And the high point of the day came when a corps of British deserters were "taken into the service of the continent."

That night John Adams strolled the city streets to enjoy what he called "the most splendid illumination I ever saw." But John did not fail to note that candles were conspicuously absent from the windows of the Tory homes. "A few surly windows were dark," he says, "but the lights were very universal."

In July, 1777, Independence could still march, glad and free, in the streets of Philadelphia and fly her American flag on high. But not so in September. On September 26, it was the Redcoats who marched the cobbled streets of the nation's capital, and the British flag that flapped aloft.

Probably there was no nook nor cranny in Independence Hall that escaped the prying eyes of the King's men, but they found no Declaration of Independence. And of all the succulent tidbits in the world, the most juicy and delectable morsel for the British lion to swallow at a gulp would have been the original parchment copy of the Declaration. That piece of parchment was the spirit of '76 made visible and tangible. To anyone who hated the ideas embodied in the document, it would have given exquisite satisfaction to destroy or treat with indignity the tangible evidence of America's will to be free and independent.

Some ten days before Philadelphia fell to the British, Congress had sent its secret journals, war records and other precious state papers (including of course the Declaration of Independence) to a small town some distance away. The delegates would have liked to send also the many bells of the city, for they knew that once in enemy hands, the bells would be melted and made into bullets. The big State House bell alone would provide an appalling number of bullets. But the delegates had no authority to direct the affairs of Philadelphia—all they could do was to send for the Supreme Executive Council of Pennsylvania and "recommend" the immediate removal of all bells in public places.

For the most part the Council agreed, although some of the gentlemen declared that if the chimes of Christ Church were taken down from the steeple, they might never find a person capable of putting them up again. These gentlemen advised doing nothing "until there is a greater probability of General Howe's getting here."

Fortunately their advice was not heeded, and under the date, September 25, 1777, is listed this item:

"To Evan and Allison, for taking down bells in the City of Philadelphia £92, 17*s.*, 6*d.*"

The State House bell (not yet known by its name *Liberty Bell*) and the chimes of Christ Church were carted off to be hidden under the flooring of a church in Allentown.

But the members of Congress lingered on. Doubtless mindful of their unnecessary flight to Baltimore, they were determined to stand by their guns up to the last possible moment.

On the night of September 19, a mounted messenger clattered noisily through the streets of Philadelphia. In his pocket was a letter from Alexander Hamilton, stating that the enemy was in possession of the ford over the Schuylkill, and might invade the capital before morning.

The president of Congress lost no time in notifying the delegates.

As John Adams expressed it, "The Congress were alarmed in their beds."

In fact, all Philadelphia was roused by the news and soon began pouring into the moon-flooded streets. Word spread that the enemy would surely burn the town—and even the Tories were frightened at that.

John and Samuel Adams set off on horseback in the company of other delegates.

Of this trip John says in part:

"From Easton we went to Bethlehem, from thence to Reading, from thence to Lancaster, and from thence to this town [York], which is about a dozen miles over the Susquehanna River. Here Congress is to sit. In order to convey the papers [official documents] with safety, which are of more importance than all the members, we were induced to take this circuit, which is near a hundred and eighty miles, whereas this town, by direct road, is not more than eighty-eight miles from Philadelphia."

On the whole Mr. Adams appears to have been enjoying himself for he added, "This tour has given me an opportunity of seeing many parts of this country which I never saw before."

In York, with a good wide river between them and the enemy, Congress, in a fairly calm state of mind, settled itself to the task of dealing with the problems of the moment.

Philadelphia did not fall, as Hamilton predicted, "before morning." It was not till six days later, on September 26, that the Redcoats arrived. But in any case, the capital city capitulated without firing a shot and that fact worried a great many people. In a letter to John, Abigail Adams said:

"I was greatly surprised when I heard that the enemy was in possession of Philadelphia, without any engagement on our part. If men will not fight and defend their own particular spot, if they will not drive the enemy from their doors, they deserve the slavery and subjection which awaits them."

But John's letter in reply threw no light on the situation. By now he had become far too cautious to trust any military information or state secrets to the doubtful safety of a letter. He merely sought to reassure Abigail by telling her that "Mr. Howe will scarcely venture upon winter quarters in Philadelphia."

This time, however, Mr. Adams proved himself a false prophet, for the British did stay all winter—in fact, they stayed in Philadelphia for nine months.

With its capital city in the hands of the enemy the military outlook for America was admittedly dark, yet not utterly black. There was a ray of hope on the horizon.

"We have had Rumours," wrote John Adams in October, "which lift us to the Stars."

The amazing "Rumours"—if true—would lift the drooping confidence of the whole country to a new high point. Unconfirmed reports had it that the Americans in the north had won a decisive victory at Saratoga—General Burgoyne and his entire army had been forced to surrender to General Gates!

The excited inhabitants of York could not wait the arrival of the messenger from General Gates. Sight unseen they fell to celebrating furiously, ringing the bells of the town "for hours." But Congress already knew the bitterness of accepting joyful rumors at face value and then finding them false. The members were extremely uneasy and full of doubt; John Adams complained of the "tormenting uncertainty concerning our affairs to the northward."

Day after day dragged on without one word from General Gates. The clouds of gloom which presently enveloped the gentlemen of Congress were rivaled only by the dense blackness of the sky over York. Rain fell in torrents. The streets turned into rivers and the fields became lakes. There hadn't been such a downpour for years.

It was ten days or more before the young colonel bearing dispatches from General Gates did finally arrive. The ringing of joy bells had not, after all, been premature, for the official report actually confirmed even the most optimistic rumors. Thereupon Congress enthusiastically recommended that a day be set apart for thanksgiving by the whole countryside. The President of Congress himself seized a pen and assured General Gates that the "glorious intelligence" was being speeded from city to city to bring joy to the heart of every loyal American.

There was some questioning in Congress concerning why the messenger had been so very slow in reaching York. The young colonel attempted to explain the delay by saying that while on the way he had been overcome by an attack of "convulsive colic." It was whispered about, however, that it was not his stomach but his heart that had suffered an attack. A certain fair maiden, with whom the colonel was in love, lived somewhere along the way and he had stopped off at her house in the hope of winning her hand.

Be that as it may, Congress was too happy over the good tidings to be very critical of the bringer, so the youthful colonel was rewarded by promotion in rank. Sam Adams, however, dryly remarked that if Congress had presented the young man with a pair of spurs, it might have been more appropriate.

The victory at Saratoga would prove of greater importance than anyone realized at the time, for it led directly to the much desired alliance with France.

For months past Congress had anxiously been waiting for word from Benjamin Franklin and Silas Deane, who were in Paris for the express purpose of inducing France to enter the war on the side of the Americans. But the two gentlemen had met with little success. The king of France was in no hurry to recognize the United States. What if, in the end, the States proved to be only thirteen defeated British colonies—France was playing safe, and why not? From her side of the Atlantic, France watched the contest with keen interest. She would concede that the rugged American volunteers had shown amazing spirit in battle, but until they could prove themselves a fair match for the well-drilled, well-supplied armies of the British and their hired German troops, she hesitated to join forces with the young experimental nation. Nevertheless guns, ammunition and even money were being shipped from France across the Atlantic for the use of the Americans—all unofficially of course.

The English minister in Paris knew very well what was happening and protested vigorously. He reminded the French of their treaty obligations to Great Britain and demanded that the shipments be stopped.

So? The French Government was filled with amazement. If such illegal shipments were indeed being sent in secret, the Government, though deeply regretful, could not of course be held responsible. Discreet French officials continued to look the other way. They saw no ships loaded with cannon and military supplies sailing without hindrance from their ports. Not they.

But with the arrival in Paris of the news of decisive victory at Saratoga, the diplomatic tide began to turn quite openly. On February 6, 1778, France took that all-important step which would materially hasten the final success of the Americans.

In England, the surrender of General Burgoyne was considered a disaster; and when on top of this, France entered the field as an ally of the American "Colonies," British royal government decided that the time was ripe for proposals of peace with Americans—peace, that is, on English terms.

And—preposterous as it may seem in our day—all this time Congress knew nothing about what was happening abroad. Not a word did they get from Franklin or his colleague—the two gentlemen might be dead for aught they knew. Congress worried and wondered. As a matter of fact Franklin had sent many a report to Congress, but every single scrap of his writing had been intercepted by the clever British.

Then, straight upon their blank ignorance of what was going on in France came another of those unconfirmed rumors to plague the gentlemen of Congress. It was said that peace commissioners from Great Britain had arrived in Philadelphia. Likely they would propose peace at a ruinous price.

America wanted no compromise peace. In fact America was determined that peace terms should not even be discussed until Great Britain had recognized the independence of the United States. But suppose things began to go from bad to worse for the Americans in the field of battle —it might be very difficult, perhaps impossible, to withstand British peace offers no matter what the terms. That was the dark side of the picture. On the other hand, suppose the British were proposing peace because France had "ratified our independence."

Good statesmen, like good detectives, have a talent for putting two and two together. England was waving an olive branch because France had promised to go all out for the Americans. In this case it was George Washington who summed up correctly.

Fortunately, the long-awaited word from the commissioners was even then on its way. On Saturday, May 2, a messenger bearing the precious state papers—treaties with France—arrived in York. Congress was not in session. Its weary members were taking a weekend off, but a hasty summons brought them all trooping back to the assembly hall to listen to the reading of the treaties. Safe to say, never was a vacation cut short with less regret. Here was an event to be celebrated with heart-felt joy, for they believed—and rightly—that the independence of the United States was now assured.

To the British in Philadelphia, the news of the alliance brought far different emotions. Consternation reigned and it needed only the hint that the French fleet would soon blockade the Delaware River (thus bottling up the troops) to set them briskly preparing to leave town. Notwithstanding their haste, the retreating army paused long enough to gather up a vast train of carts loaded with booty.

Tory citizens of Philadelphia who had been hand in

glove with the dashing young Redcoats, holding festivity in their honor, were now in a panic. They feared being on hand when the American troops marched into Philadelphia and returning citizens discovered the damage done their city. The capital was not destroyed, but it had been ruthlessly defaced and plundered. There would be fierce resentment and perhaps retaliation—the Tories had no mind to face the consequences. They took the alternative and by the hundreds, they trailed along after the evacuating army. Irate Philadelphians might vent their anger on the less cautious.

Indeed there was cause for anger. The fine old State House in particular had suffered grievously. The British had used it as a hospital for wounded prisoners of war. One of the returning delegates described its appalling condition with disgust. He wrote of the "offensiveness of the air in and about the State House which the Enemy had made an Hospital and left in a condition disgraceful to the Character of civility."

After extensive repairs and vigorous scouring with soap and sand, the much-abused building was again ready to house Congress.

Delegate John Adams was not among the members who returned to Philadelphia in July. Early in the winter Congress had appointed him Joint Commissioner to the Court of France and in February, 1778, he had sailed from Boston, taking with him his small son, John Quincy Adams, age ten. Poor Abigail would now have two absent members of her family to worry about—and with good reason. Unquestionably, the small frigate from New England was in grave danger of being captured by British warships. Months must pass before a letter could reach her telling of the safe arrival of the two travelers. But in time that letter did arrive.

As delegate from Massachusetts, there would be no more sessions in Congress for John Adams. For years to come he would continue to serve his country from abroad.

18

We, the People

Early in September, 1781, the streets of Philadelphia were a-clatter with the noise of tramping boots; and from the windows and doorway of the State House, the gentlemen of Congress watched with delight the procession of French troops. Their white uniforms gleamed like snow in the sun and they marched with a rhythmic precision that greatly impressed the spectators.

The troops of our ally and the army of General Washington were heading southward—that much was obvious. But not even Congress knew that the General hoped, with the aid of the French fleet, to trap Cornwallis in Virginia —a hope that was presently realized.

Little more than a month later Cornwallis was indeed trapped in Yorktown—penned in between the combined French and American armies on one side, and an overwhelming French naval force on the other.

On the nineteenth of October the British commander surrendered.

A hard-riding messenger, carrying the news to Congress, reached Philadelphia in record time, arriving about 3:00 A.M. on Monday, October 22. What though all the city slept at that unearthly hour, when Washington's courier rode through its dark streets, the news he bore was no respecter of sleep. Even the stolid night watchman trudging his dreary rounds must needs shout the news of British surrender. Philadelphia awoke as one man.

Excited patriots could not wait till dawn to celebrate, they must build huge bonfires, ring bells and shout themselves hoarse. For this was no ordinary victory. The surrender of Cornwallis and his whole army tipped the scales of war in America's favor. There would be no more fighting on American soil, but that did not mean that peace would automatically follow. Far from it.

There arose various diplomatic complications. England and France were still at war with each other, their respective fleets battling on the high seas. France was America's ally and under such conditions America was not supposed to make a separate peace with England. Furthermore, George III still refused to give official recognition to the new status of the thirteen united States and until the stubborn king yielded that point America was determined not to be bound by any terms.

Meantime, however, Congress could and did appoint commissioners—John Adams among others—to work out a provisional treaty of peace. The Peace Conference met in Paris in the winter of 1781-82, but progress was discouragingly slow, and it was not until November, 1782, that an agreement was finally reached and the preliminary articles were actually signed.

In America, Congress impatiently awaited official report from the commissions, but as so frequently happened, instead of dependable word only mystifying rumors drifted irresponsibly across the ocean to cause confusion and concern. One such report from France declared that negotiations had broken down completely and the war must go on. Anxious New Yorkers besieged the stages coming from Philadelphia, in the hope of getting the latest news from Congress, but Congress itself had had no news. As one of the members said, "It is now five months since we have received any dispatches from Europe, and all private accounts from any quarter are vague and not much depended on."

At length the deadlock was broken in March, 1783, by the arrival of the official dispatches and the provisional treaty duly signed by the ministers of Great Britain and the United States.

The long war had lasted almost eight full years and Congress, with one eye on the calendar, appointed April 19, the eighth anniversary of the "accident" on Lexington Green, as the day on which to issue its formal Proclamation of Peace with Great Britain.

Peace with Great Britain—yes—but how about peace at home?

Peace, in the national sense of the word, is not miraculously born when the shooting stops, much as we should like to think so. During the war, the States had all been bound together by their mutual rebellion against British despotism. They all felt the same way. But when despotism ceased, that bond of sympathy was gone. Each State began to look out for number one. Its own immediate interests became paramount; and of course that attitude of mind made not for united States, but for dis-united states. Local prejudices and petty jealousies grew like weeds.

The States were about as peaceful as the proverbial Kilkenny cats.

Only a few men, George Washington among them, had the wit to see that the true and vital interests of the thirteen States were identical, that co-operation would bring better results for all.

Meanwhile there was no real government. Continental Congress continued to wrestle with the gigantic problem of how a country could be free and yet at the same time, subject to reasonable control. As yet there was no efficient machinery of government, and indeed Congress had small power to enforce any control over the States that were running wild, like children too suddenly given liberty without responsibility. Apparently it was Congress who must take on its feeble shoulders all the responsibility, and this without legal authority to enforce law. The situation was impossible.

Congress was helpless and the members began staying away in droves. Often it was difficult to get even the necessary quorum to vote on any measure. And all the while dissension among the States grew until it reached such a pitch that certain of them threatened to secede.

After all that the new nation had suffered, after all the sacrifices and agonies it had so bravely met in defense of the high ideals of freedom, it dropped down to this low level—that the thirteen States were squabbling among themselves even to the verge of civil war.

So obvious was this sorry plight that the States themselves saw their own danger and Congress willingly fell in with a proposal that a convention be held for the express purpose of drawing up a plan of "federal government adequate to the exigencies of the Union." And all the States, with the exception of Rhode Island, approved the idea and appointed "deputies" to represent them at the convention, which would be held in Philadelphia in May, 1787.

The fifty-five deputies who foregathered in the high, white-paneled room in the old State House were indeed a representative group. Of course there were many lawyers, but there were also merchants, ministers, physicians, soldiers and planters. Forty of them had, at one time or another, been members of the Continental Congress and of these, eight had signed the Declaration of Independence—and in that same room.

However, the author of that famous document was not present, nor was the man who had so valiantly encouraged its adoption. Both Thomas Jefferson and John Adams were abroad, serving as America's official representatives.

But Benjamin Franklin was present, despite his advanced age of eighty-one, so was George Washington. Washington was unanimously elected President of the Convention.

Like the delegates of the Continental Congress, the deputies met behind locked doors, but unlike the delegates, the gentlemen of the Federal Convention kept their debates so secret that no details concerning the sessions reached the ears of the curious public. But it was no secret that the deputies did not see eye to eye—to put it mildly.

Certain of them were bent on patching up the old machinery of government—revising the Articles of Confederation and letting it go at that—while other, wiser men saw the need to devise a strong plan of national government which would rest not merely on the States as individual communities, but rather on the people as a whole.

During all that hot and humid summer the deputies wrestled with their difficult task. At times it seemed as though the conflict of ideas could lead only to an open break. Deputies from the smaller States formed a group, opposing the large-State group; and southern States lined up against northern States. Nevertheless, a compromise plan was finally agreed upon.

By now the fifty-five deputies had dwindled to forty-two.

Unlike the Declaration, the draft of the Constitution seems not to have been written by one man alone. Instead, the approved material was turned over to a Committee of Style, who polished and clarified it. Then after the revised text had been submitted to the Convention, it was given to an expert penman "to transcribe & engross."

This engrosser had ideas of his own concerning capitals, spelling and punctuation—sometimes he began nouns with capital letters, sometimes he merely enlarged a small letter; but doubtless he more than earned the sum of thirty dollars, said to have been paid him, for he had to pen well over four thousand words.

The formalities of signing the parchment copy of the Constitution were similar to those attending the signing of the Declaration—but with one marked difference—emotional tension was lacking. No signer of the Constitution was risking his life by writing his name beneath it. In fact, his signature was being added to a document which might not even be accepted by the States. Unless and until two-thirds of the thirteen States ratified the proposed Constitution, it was nothing but a plan on parchment.

The signature of Washington came first—written thus:

G° Washington—Presd.ᵗ
and deputy from Virginia

Beneath it came the signatures of thirty-nine of the deputies, grouped according to States. Three disapproving gentlemen refused point-blank to sign.

It was now late September and the document must first be formally presented to Continental Congress, then published and offered to the States for their consideration.

With its publication a storm of controversy was let loose. Every citizen in the land, it appeared, had an opinion to express. The shortcomings and good features of the proposed constitution were the chief topic of conversation wherever people gathered. Shops, taverns, town meetings, even churches, rang with talk of the pros and cons of what was called a "bundle of compromises."

Samuel Adams, in Boston, hesitated to give his approval, so too did John Hancock. In Virginia, Patrick Henry and Robert Henry Lee were strongly opposed to ratification; but George Washington flatly stated his belief that a second Convention could produce no better results. He declared that all arguments against the Constitution were "addressed to the passions of the people and obviously calculated to alarm their fears."

"The people" undoubtedly did have fears. They wanted to see, in black and white, the promise that the new government would make no laws of intolerance concerning religion, or prohibit freedom of speech, or freedom of the press. They wanted to make sure of their *right* "to petition the government for a redress of grievances." They wanted to make sure no soldiers would ever again be quartered in their homes. In short, they wanted no return of tyranny in any way, shape or manner.

So a form of definite reassurance was devised which would do away with their objections and open the way for ratification. This was the proposal of amendments—a bill of rights.

Little Delaware was the first State to ratify, and by unanimous vote. Five days later, on December 12, 1887, Pennsylvania followed suit despite the strong opposition vote of twenty-three members who voted nay. By the end of the following June, ten States had ratified the Constitution—exactly one more than was needed for the two-thirds vote. Rhode Island continued to cling stubbornly to her isolationist stand. She had refused to send deputies to the Convention, and she refused to ratify the plan of national government. In fact, it took Rhode Island a very long time to join her sister States.

From the far side of the Atlantic John Adams was keeping in touch with the trend of affairs at home as best he could. And when, in the fall of 1787, the controversy over the Constitution broke out, John—who was all for the document—reacted in a most characteristic manner. He seized his pen and wrote. He wrote at such long length that when published, his *Defense of the Constitution of the United States* filled three volumes.

At this time John Adams was minister to Great Britain. All told, he had been ten years in foreign service and he now felt that he had earned the right to retire. So, at his own urgent request, Congress accepted his resignation and John was free to return home.

The Mr. Adams who took ship for America was an older, wiser and somewhat plumper gentleman than the "fire-eater" of prewar days. His political enemies—and there were many of them—had nicknamed him "His Rotundity." To this staunch New Englander, retirement probably meant settling down in peace and comfort on his pleasant farm in Braintree. But as he was to discover, instead of enjoying the quiet life of a country gentleman, he would soon find himself serving as his country's first Vice President. Following two full terms in that office, John Adams would himself be advanced to the presidency.

With the ratification of the Constitution in the early summer of 1788, a page in American history was turned. Continental Congress had served to the best of its ability for fifteen difficult years, and now a new form of government must take over. Little remained for the retiring Congress to do, beyond directing that on "the first Wednesday in Jany next" the States appoint Electors who on "the first Wednesday in feby. next . . . vote for a president." And that "the first Wednesday in March next be the time and the present seat of [Continental] Congress the place for commencing proceedings under the said constitution."

The proceedings scheduled to commence on Wednesday, March 4, 1789, at "the present seat" of the old Congress in New York, were delayed a little. The new President, George Washington, was not inaugurated until the thirtieth of April. New York had been the seat of government since 1785 and the idea of becoming the permanent capital greatly appealed to New Yorkers. But in 1790, government again pulled up stakes and moved back to Philadelphia.

Once again George Washington, John Adams and Thomas Jefferson—the latter now Secretary of State—would stroll across the large square behind the State House. But doubtless none of the gentlemen would any longer refer to the square as "the Yard," for the old State House Yard was now known as Independence Square, a place of green lawns and shade trees. In the northeast corner of the square stood Congress Hall, the present seat of government, and here Washington's second inauguration would take place. Here too, John Adams and Thomas Jefferson would take the oath of office in 1797, when Adams became President and Jefferson, Vice President. The dignified old Congress Hall still stands, a fitting neighbor to historic Independence Hall.

By the time John Adams became President, plans for a permanent national capital had long been under way. In 1791, Congress had authorized President Washington to select the site for the new capital, which was to bear his name. The spot he chose was not a city, but a sparsely settled tract of lowland on the left bank of the Potomac. In such a spot the new capital could be built from the ground up, without the handicap of a previously built city. Nevertheless, the task was much like creating order out of chaos.

By 1800, wide streets and broad avenues had been staked out and a few public buildings nearly completed—there was at least the beginning of a city—so government transferred its important State papers, including the Declaration of Independence, to the new capitol. And in the autumn President Adams and Congress moved to "the city" on the Potomac.

Said one letter-writer: "The Capitol is on an eminence near the center of the immense country called here the city. There is one good tavern and several other houses are finished or being built."

"The city" was also known as "The Capital of Miserable Huts," and "The City of Streets Without Houses." On paper the plans for the many streets were most impressive, but for the most part these fine highways existed only on paper and one was forced to travel over rough roads, heavy with mud in which the local livestock, particularly pigs, delighted to wallow.

The new nation was indeed having its full share of troubles in setting up housekeeping.

19

The Burning of the Capitol

The city of Washington, brand new capital of the United States of America, had been carefully planned by an expert. It was to be the most beautiful city in the world. But in the year 1800, cities did not spring into existence overnight like mushrooms. Nevertheless, it seems that government was eager to move into its new abode as soon as there might be a roof over its head. The presidential mansion and certain of the public buildings were thought to be, if not completed, at least habitable.

Accordingly, on Monday, October 15, President John Adams accompanied by the First Lady of the Land, set out from Boston for their new home, traveling by coach. The early stages of the journey south, although tiring, were uneventful and all went well enough with the presidential party until it came within forty miles of its destination.

Shortly after leaving Baltimore the road began to meander uncertainly through the wilderness until gradually all semblance to a traveled route vanished. The driver of the coach became bewildered and was finally forced to admit that he was hopelessly lost. The travelers had not taken the precaution to hire a guide, so there they were, the President and his Lady, as lost as the babes in the woods. But luck was with them, for ere long they chanced upon a Negro slave who was able to point out the way, and thus, says John Adams, "we were extricated from the woods."

Without further mishap they reached their new abode. But alas for the first mistress of the first presidential mansion in Washington! House-keeping as well as government could present most difficult problems.

In a letter to her daughter, Abigail confessed that "the principal stairs are not up, and will not be this winter." She called the mansion "this great castle," and sighed over the need to keep fires going in the many rooms for the sake of driving out the dampness and "secure us from daily agues." But try as she might the poor lady could not get sufficient wood for her fires, "because people cannot be found to cut and cart it," in spite of the forests close at hand.

Mrs. Adams consoled herself with the thought that in a few months' time she would be returning north, leaving the vexatious problem of heating "the castle" to the new President. On March 4, 1801, Thomas Jefferson would take office.

When the original copy of the Declaration of Independence had been transferred from Philadelphia to the new and (presumably) permanent quarters in Washington, D.C., the yellowing parchment was already crisscrossed with many tiny cracks. It was only a quarter of a century old, which is really no age at all for parchment. Its worn appearance was due not to age, but rather to frequent handling. Never during its troubled history had the precious document been allowed to remain long in any one place. Even in brief review the record of its many journeys is impressive.

First there was that hurried trip from Philadelphia to Baltimore, when an over-cautious Congress fled the city with all the state papers, only to return a few weeks later. The next flight was necessary enough, for the British soon thereafter did capture Philadelphia. In the fall of that same year—1777—the document and other state records were sent by roundabout route to Lancaster, then to York; and following the evacuation of Philadelphia by the enemy in 1778, the papers were carried back to that city. In 1783, Congress proclaimed the peace and presently packed up bag and baggage and moved officially to Annapolis. The following year it transferred the seat of government to Trenton, and in 1785, it moved on to New York City. Four years later the State Department of the new national government assumed responsibility for the state papers, and in 1790, carried them to Philadelphia. In 1800 came the move to the new capital, Washington, D.C.

But the record of journeys does not end in 1800. After fourteen years came another period of danger when the much-handled document must again be dragged forth and sent fleeing from capture by British troops. This time to escape only by a hair's breadth. Twenty-nine years after the war-torn young nation had signed a peace treaty with Great Britain, the two of them were at it again, trying to fight their way to an understanding.

The War of 1812 was no sudden outbreak. It came only after a long succession of encroachments. Even during Jefferson's administration there was grave danger of America's becoming involved in war with France or with England. No American merchantman could sail the seas in safety. Napoleon seized our ships and stole our cargoes. England seized our ships and ruthlessly removed all seamen "believed" to have been born on British soil. The British navy needed every able-bodied seaman it could get by hook or crook, because England was then at war with France.

In 1809, Madison succeeded Jefferson as President. America, trying to avoid war, was still clinging desperately to the role of neutral, although the number of American seamen impressed into British service already ran to several thousand.

But since the "Mistress of the Seas" stubbornly refused to mend her ways, America after a time, ceased to be neutral. June 1, 1812, President Madison sent a message to Congress recommending a formal declaration of war. Eighteen days later the young nation, backed by a few thousand trained troops and a very small navy was again at war with England.

For a time the little navy managed to win spectacular victories, but by midsummer, 1814, the royal fleet had invaded the Chesapeake, and British troops were within twenty miles of Washington. Yet certain officials of government would not admit that the capital was in any real danger.

General Armstrong, Secretary of War, scouted the idea of an attack on the city. "Have they artillery?" he demanded, and he supplied the answer himself. "No! Have they cavalry? No. Then don't tell an old soldier that any regular army will or can come. We are more frightened than hurt, or likely to be," declared the General.

But President Madison was not convinced by the words of an "old soldier," and sent out a hurry call for a special meeting of his cabinet. Nor did Colonel Monroe, Secretary of State, agree with the General.

For several days the Colonel had been doing a bit of reconnoitering on his own. He was in no mind to risk the capture, by the British, of such treasured documents as the Constitution and the Declaration, so in spite of the General's arguments, he again mounted his horse and set forth. This time he rode out to a little village on the Patuxent River, and what he found must have brought him up with a start.

Boatload after boatload of British soldiers were being landed. Obviously an attack was imminent.

Colonel Monroe immediately scribbled a note to General S. Pleasonton, directing him to "take the best possible care" of the books and papers in the office of the State Department. This note he gave to a messenger to be delivered in haste.

Now General Pleasonton was not a man to sit cogitating, hand on brow, while he considered whether or not the enemy had artillery and cavalry. Instead, he hurried off to buy some coarse linen to be made into bags of a size he briefly describes as "convenient."

By Sunday morning, August 21, the city of Washington rang with the dire threat: "The British are coming!"

That phrase had not lost its power to terrorize the citizens. Suddenly the capital resolved itself into the semblance of a disturbed ant hill. The people poured from their houses into the streets, first snatching up anything at hand in the way of personal possessions. Those who were fortunate enough to own carriages, loaded them with furniture; but for carrying small belongings, anything on wheels—even the lowly wheelbarrow—came in handy. Thus loaded down with a most diverse assortment of articles, the populace fled the city.

On Capitol Hill, the government clerks were furiously packing up office records. General Pleasonton, aided by the chief clerk of the State Department, hurriedly stuffed records and documents into his "convenient" sized linen bags. While he was thus engaged, the Secretary of War, whose office was directly across the hall, opened his door and stood glaring at these activities with disapproval.

To General Armstrong's mind, all this alarm was quite "unnecessary." He said that he *still* did not think the British were serious. "They do not intend to come to Washington," he insisted.

But General Pleasonton was not to be deterred. This was no time for argument.

"We are under a different belief," he told General Armstrong, "and let their intentions be what they may, it is the part of prudence to preserve the valuable papers of the Revolutionary Government."

Chief among these papers were "the secret journals of Continental Congress (not yet published), the correspondence of General Washington, the laws, and the Declaration of Independence."

When the last book of records had been packed, the heavy bags were loaded into carts and the little train, with General Pleasonton in charge, set off for a certain grist

THE·FLIGHT·FROM·WASHINGTON

mill which was "situated," he says, "a short distance on the Virginia side of the Potomac, beyond the chain-bridge, so called, two miles above Georgetown."

On reaching the mill, the General seems to have paused for reconsideration. He didn't like the look of things. The mill was not being used at the time, and the idea of trusting the precious papers to the questionable protection of the ramshackle building held no appeal. He knew there was danger that British scouting parties might ransack the neighborhood; and as hiding place the old mill did not look so good.

Apparently the General also found his carts not so good.

"I proceeded to some farm houses in Virginia," he says, "and procured wagons, in which the books and papers were deposited."

He then started for Leesburg, thirty-five miles away.

In Leesburg the General discovered just the sort of place he was looking for—an unoccupied house with a stout, lockable door. So the heavy bags were presently stowed safely away, the door locked and the key turned over to the Reverend Mr. Littlejohn.

By this time, says the General, he was thoroughly tired and quite ready to retire at an early hour. And so forthwith he did retire.

Doubtless after such a day the General slept heavily, for he never woke up during all the commotion in the tavern that night. He did not hear the sound of boots hurriedly clumping down the stairs, nor the excited voices of people in the street. It was not until morning that he learned what had happened.

Early in the night the sky in the direction of Washington

had turned rosy and then glared with ominous red. At times the light flared high and then appeared to be blanketed in clouds of heavy smoke. The watchers in Leesburg could hear an occasional heavy roar, like the sound of exploding powder magazines. Toward morning came a sudden storm and everyone was forced to seek shelter indoors.

So violent was the wind that trees were uprooted and roofs whipped off sheds. But the storm did not last very long. Overhead the sky cleared, but not in the direction of Washington—there it remained a dense mass of black. And no one could doubt what that meant.

All this happened on Wednesday night, August 21.

On Thursday night the British withdrew from Washington, leaving behind them desolation and ruin. And when, on Friday, General Pleasonton rode back to the capital, he found "the President's house and the public buildings were still burning."

The British had entered and taken possession of the city even while the General and his wagons were on the road to Leesburg.

According to the account given by one British narrator, the royal troops had taken the city without a struggle; and just at sunset, on Wednesday, they had begun their "task" of destroying the capital. He describes with great relish "the blazing houses, ships and stores, the reports of exploding magazines and crash of falling roofs." The narrator is moved to dramatic eloquence:

"The sky was brilliantly illuminated by the different conflagrations," he says, "and a dark, red light was thrown upon the road, sufficient to permit each man to view distinctly his comrade's face. . . . Toward morning, a violent storm of rain with thunder and lightning, came on, whose flashes seemed to vie in brilliancy with the flames which burst from the roofs of burning houses, while the thunder drown the noise of crumbling walls, and was only interrupted by the occasional roar of cannon, and of large deposits of gun-powder, as they exploded one by one."

Not even that "violent storm of rain" before dawn on Thursday was enough to quench the flames. More than twenty-four hours later, General Pleasonton would find the public buildings still burning.

With the Capitol in ruins, many worried citizens of Washington now believed that the seat of government would never again return. Nor were their fears dispelled after they had gone to see with their own eyes what was left of the public buildings.

In a letter to a friend one lady of Washington wrote:

"Those beautiful pillars in that Representatives Hall were crack'd and broken, the roof, that noble dome, painted and carved with such beauty and skill, lay in ashes in the cellars beneath the smoldering ruins, [which] were yet smoking. In the P.H. [President's House] not an inch, but its crack'd and blacken'd walls remain'd."

It soon became common knowledge that the President and other officials of government were holding their meetings in Fredericktown. That this should have become necessary, because Washington had been destroyed, with no attempt whatsoever at defense, enraged the citizens. The overconfident Secretary of War especially was blamed.

Wrote one angry citizen: "Universal execration follows Armstrong, who it is believed never wished to defend the city and I was assured that had he pass'd thro' the city the day after the engagement, he would have been torn to pieces."

Public indignation reached such a pitch that Secretary Armstrong was presently forced to resign from office.

General Pleasonton's report makes no mention of this flood of wrath. He merely says that "it was not considered safe to bring the papers of the State Department back to Washington for some weeks, not indeed, until the British fleet generally had left the waters of the Chesapeake. In the meantime, it was necessary for me to proceed to Leesburg occasionally, for particular papers, to which the Secretary of State had occasion to refer in the course of his correspondence."

There never was any serious doubt as to the rebuilding of the Capitol. In the course of a few years the public buildings and the President's House rose again to stand triumphant, the hub of a growing city.

For many years to come the original parchment copy of the Declaration rested undisturbed in the Treasury Building in Washington. Then in 1833 came another near-catastrophe. Fire destroyed the Treasury Building but not the precious document, which was hastily rescued. It remained in the custody of the State Department until 1841 and at that date was deposited in the Patent Office. Some years later the document would set forth on another journey, not a flight by cart, but a journey by rail in all the well-guarded dignity of its priceless value.

20

The Fiftieth Anniversary

When the fiftieth birthday of our nation drew near, the two great Americans so directly connected with the emancipation of their country —John Adams and Thomas Jefferson—were still living.

John Adams's last years were spent in his beloved New England, where in fair weather, this stocky, energetic old gentleman would tramp the hills, walking as far as three or four miles at a stretch. He still rode horseback "now and again," he says, but rarely more than "ten or fifteen miles."

Braintree was now known as Quincy, and it was here that John Adams and his family still had their home. Every holiday would bring to the homestead a flock of grandchildren—thirteen of them—and several great-grandchildren as well. Naturally the old statesman took great pride in the political career of his eldest son, John Quincy Adams; and John, senior, would live long enough to see John, junior, elected to the presidency in 1825.

Like John Adams, Jefferson also was to spend the closing years of his life in the place, above all others, where he preferred to be. It was with wholehearted relief that Jefferson had retired from public service. For the first time in his long life he was free to settle down for good and for all at Monticello.

This did not mean that he would cease to take an active interest in the affairs of his country, nor that he would lose touch with what was going on in Washington. Far from it. The two Presidents, Madison and Monroe, who held office for the next sixteen years, were his close friends and usually turned to him for counsel whenever new and difficult problems of government were under consideration.

Jefferson, ten years younger than John Adams, was still a vigorous man when he retired from public life. Besides managing his mountaintop plantation, which he said, kept him "mostly on horseback" from breakfast till sundown, he kept an eye on his other estate, "Poplar Forest," some eighty miles distant. This meant riding those eighty miles and back again at least four times a year.

But in spite of all this supervision of his personal affairs, Jefferson yet found time to give heed to the future of the young nation. A matter which deeply concerned him was the education of the people.

America was now free and independent—that goal had already been won, but another progressive step was necessary. Freedom and independence must not be left to the dubious guardianship of ignorance and stupidity. Since government now lay in the hands of the people, the people must be educated in order to govern themselves with intelligence.

To this end Jefferson worked out plans for better and more wide-spread schooling. To some extent he was able, during his lifetime, to carry out these plans. He not only reorganized the course of study in the University of Virginia, but in his capacity of architect, drew the plans for the building of the new University of Virginia.

During a period of political storm and stress there occurred a break in the friendship between Adams and Jefferson—a misunderstanding it was, but no relentless feud —for after a time the breach was mended and the bonds of sympathy were never again broken. With advancing years the touchy, quick-tempered John Adams grew more mellow, and came to value beyond price the friendship of Jefferson. As often as possible the two men exchanged letters, and even though the distance which lay between Massachusetts and Virginia might prevent their meeting in the flesh, it is obvious from their letters that they drew ever closer in spirit.

As the Fourth of July, 1826, was approaching, the citizens of Quincy began planning an impressive celebration. In the opinion of the committee in charge, nothing could be more fitting for the occasion than a public speech by the oldest surviving signer of the Declaration of Independence.

But John Adams assured the committee that he had no desire to make "a last public appearance." He would, however, suggest a toast which could be presented as coming from him.

"I will give you," said he, *Independence Forever.*

The committee wanted more. Wouldn't Mr. Adams add something?

"Not a word," said John.

While John Adams was dealing with the committee in

Quincy; at Monticello, Thomas Jefferson lay ill in his bed. Too ill to be asked to take any part in the coming celebration of the national holiday. Nevertheless, the thought of that great day was in his heart.

He would leave one deathless word for the new nation —one word, sealed with his signature. For the last time in his life, he took up his pen and wrote:

Freedom. Thomas Jefferson.

When the sun rose on the Fourth of July, 1826, it found America joyously celebrating its fiftieth birthday. Before the sun went down on that same day, it looked upon joy turned to sorrow. But deeper than sorrow lay great wonder, for the day was woven of coincidence so strange that all the history of the world can scarcely offer a parallel.

On the Fourth of July, exactly half a century from the day on which the Declaration of Independence was adopted, the man who wrote it and the man who so ardently backed it—Thomas Jefferson and John Adams—both died, almost within the hour.

Both died, each leaving to the new nation a last message, which, the two being combined, reads:

Freedom and Independence Forever.

When the news of the day's happenings spread through the land, the people were filled with awe and amazement. They looked upon this most unusual concurrence of events as some manner of sign or portent, though what it signified was not clear to them.

Call it superstition if you will, but in itself, man's power to wonder is not a thing to be too lightly dismissed. At all

216

events, the message left to us by our founding fathers, though clearer today than ever before, is still a thing not yet all understood.

Freedom and Independence Forever.

The words are still a matter for reverent wonderment.

21

The Hundredth Anniversary

On the Fourth of July, 1876, the United States of America reached her hundredth birthday. Compared to the great nations of Europe, the U.S.A. was still an infant in the matter of years, but such a robust, fast-growing youngster that in many respects she was already abreast of the older nations of Europe.

Peace reigned in the land and for the younger generation of Americans, there was the beginning of that sweet delusion—a belief that the brutal and barbarous practice of settling disputes by war was a thing of the past. By 1876, progress, development, expressed the spirit of the times.

In this joyous, carefree, self-confident state of mind, with all the vigor of youth, America made ready for her centennial birthday party. It was her "coming-out party" and all the world was invited to attend. Naturally, Philadelphia, birthplace of American independence, was the city where the celebration would take place.

Since 1876, America has staged a number of gigantic and extravagant expositions, but up to that date there had been nothing to match this one on our side of the Atlantic, and the Centennial Exposition was considered the last word in the way of a stupendous show. In praise of its glories, contemporary writers exhausted their entire vocabulary of adjectives in the superlative degree and were left helplessly gasping for words sufficiently strong to express their sentiments.

For example, one man wrote, "We cannot overstate the material magnificence of this, no matter from what point of view we regard it. Words cannot paint it; song cannot celebrate it; it is incredulous—" (he meant *incredible* but was too dazed to know it) "we believe, because it is impossible."

By the time this breathless eyewitness comes to the display of machines, it is too much for him, he is swept off the solid earth into the realms of fantasy. He says, "We walk as in a dream, confused with the forces which Labor has conjured up, spirits which it has let loose upon us—"

Yet the man who was thus overwhelmed by the "spirits let loose" by machinery, had never remotely dreamed of automobiles, radios and airplanes, let alone the thousand and one other mechanical "spirits" and gadgets of the twentieth century, for 1876 knew them not.

Even so, lacking our present day advance, the Centennial Exposition was a gorgeous, glittering affair where one could see "the wonderous display of every marvel and masterpiece gathered from art and nature in four continents." It was a "festival of oratory, music, poetry, parades, bells, illumination, regattas, cannon, banners, halleluiahs and huzzas."

In such terms did robust young America leave us report of her centennial birthday party. Strong, lighthearted and hopeful as befitted youth, U.S.A. might be tripping a gay dance one hundred years after claiming independence, but she was not quite forgetting why she was dancing.

The old causes of hatred and rebellion against English rule were stone dead. Once again America knew that England, by tie of blood, was the nearest and dearest of kin. And now, although the Declaration of Independence might no longer be considered an instrument of revolt (since there was no occasion for revolt) it was an article of political faith—the American creed to be upheld forever.

Considering these facts, there was one indispensable document which must be present at the Centennial Exposition; namely, the Declaration of Independence.

At the age of one hundred years the precious parchment was cracked, discolored and faded. So many times in the past it had traveled from pillar to post. Usually it was kept rolled up scroll-fashion, so that even apart from its hasty rough and tumble journeyings, constant rolling and unrolling had subjected it to an uncommon amount of wear and tear. But now, in 1876, the Declaration would be handled with the utmost concern for its preservation. By this time it was no longer rolled, but flattened and protected by a simple frame.

On the Fourth of July, 1876, came the climax of the Centennial Exposition—the celebration of its reason for being. For a brief time the day would be, as nearly as possible, a repetition, a flash back to 1776. The gentlemen of Congress had made a special trip from Washington to Philadelphia for the express purpose of meeting in the Declaration Chamber—the very room where one hundred years earlier the members of Continental Congress had voted to adopt Jefferson's draft of the Declaration.

As in that former day, there was a flag-draped stand in the big square behind Independence Hall and once again thousands of people stood waiting in the Square, once again the Declaration of Independence was being read aloud—read from the original document, this time by Richard Henry Lee, grandson of the Richard Henry Lee who had introduced the resolution calling for independence.

Time might fade the ink, but never the spirit of the Declaration. The listening people of 1876 were deeply moved, as had been their forefathers a hundred years earlier. And when, after the reading, Mr. Lee held aloft the old document so that all might see it, "cheer followed cheer at this rare spectacle."

At the close of the Exposition, Philadelphia was loathe to part with the historic parchment. Certain of the prominent citizens claimed that its rightful place was in Independence Hall, and it was not until the Patent Office in Washington had made several urgent requests for its return that the point was yielded and the document sent back to Washington, where it was placed on exhibition in a special cabinet in the Library of Congress.

But even that protection proved insufficient. By 1894, the ink had become so faded through continual exposure to light that the heavy signature of John Hancock was scarcely visible and very few other names could be read at all.

So the Declaration was now locked away in the protective darkness of a safe and in its place in the cabinet was set a facsimile. But a substitute, no matter how good, still left us wishing to see the original. Therefore, in 1921, the old document was again brought forth into the daylight and placed on exhibition in the Library of Congress—this time protected by amber glass, which would check further discoloration and fading.

Under such conditions it would seem that the preservation and safety of the Declaration were assured. But just as the year 1941 was drawing to a close came the bombing of Pearl Harbor. The cataclysm of war had struck our shores and no mortal could guess the final outcome.

Reacting to danger, like all men since creation, we hastened to hide from the destructive enemy the things most precious to us. America's three unreplaceable old documents—the Declaration of Independence, the Articles of Confederation, and the Constitution—were sealed in bronze cylinders, carefully boxed and shipped in secret, first to one hiding place then to another—five in all. When at length we did know the outcome of World War II, the names of four of those places were revealed. They were the University of Virginia, Washington and Lee University, Virginia Military Institute and Denison University at Granville, Ohio. The name of the fifth hiding place remains a state secret.

On October 1, 1944, the documents, having been returned to Washington, were again exhibited to public view. At present the Declaration of Independence rests in a shrine of bronze and marble in the Library of Congress.

The thirteen "united" States have multiplied into forty-eight United States, and visitors from every corner of our nation come to stand within the balustrade and look upon this symbol of American ideals. What those who look upon it feel, how deeply they are moved, depends upon the depth of their love and understanding of freedom.

IN CONGRESS, JULY 4, 1776.

THE unanimous DECLARATION of the thirteen united STATES OF AMERICA,

WHEN in the Course of human events, it becomes necessary for one people to dissolve the political bands which have connected them with another, and to assume among the powers of the earth, the separate and equal station to which the Laws of Nature and of Nature's God entitle them, a decent respect to the opinions of mankind requires that they should declare the causes which impel them to the separation.——We hold these truths to be self-evident, that all men are created equal, that they are endowed by their Creator with certain unalienable Rights, that among these are Life, Liberty and the pursuit of Happiness.——That to secure these rights, Governments are instituted among Men, deriving their just powers from the consent of the governed,——That whenever any Form of Government becomes destructive of these ends, it is the Right of the People to alter or to abolish it, and to institute new Government, laying its foundation on such principles and organizing its powers in such form, as to them shall seem most likely to effect their Safety and Happiness. Prudence, indeed, will dictate that Governments long

In the parchment copy of the Declaration, the paragraphs—with one exception—are indicated by dashes, and two slight errors are corrected by interlineation.

established should not be changed for light and transient causes; and accordingly all experience hath shewn, that mankind are more disposed to suffer, while evils are sufferable, than to right themselves by abolishing the forms to which they are accustomed. But when a long train of abuses and usurpations, pursuing invariably the same Object evinces a design to reduce them under absolute Despotism, it is their right, it is their duty, to throw off such Government, and to provide new Guards for their future security.——Such has been the patient sufferance of these Colonies; and such is now the necessity which constrains them to alter their former Systems of Government. The history of the present King of Great Britain is a history of repeated injuries and usurpations, all having in direct object the establishment of an absolute Tyranny over these States. To prove this, let Facts be submitted to a candid world.——He has refused his Assent to Laws, the most wholesome and necessary for the public good.——He has forbidden his Governors to pass Laws of immediate and pressing importance, unless suspended in their operation till his Assent should be obtained; and when so suspended, he has utterly neglected to attend to them.——He has refused to pass other Laws for the accommodation of large districts of people, unless those people would relinquish the right of Representation in the Legislature, a right inestimable to them and formidable to tyrants only.——He has called together legislative bodies at places unusual, uncomfortable, and distant from the depository of their public Records, for the sole purpose of fatiguing them into compliance with his measures.——He has dissolved Representative Houses repeatedly, for opposing with manly firmness his invasions on the rights of the people.——He has refused for a long time, after such dissolutions, to cause others to be elected; whereby the Legislative powers, incapable of Annihilation, have returned to the People at large for their exercise; the State remaining in the meantime exposed to all the dangers of invasion from without, and convulsions within.——He has endeavoured to prevent the population of these States; for that purpose obstructing the Laws for Naturalization of Foreigners; refusing to pass others to encourage their migrations hither, and raising the conditions of new Appropriations of Lands.——He has obstructed the Administration of Justice, by refusing his Assent to Laws for establishing Judiciary powers.——He has made Judges dependent on his Will alone, for the tenure of their offices, and the amount and payment of their salaries.——He has erected a multitude of New Offices, and sent hither swarms of Officers to harrass our people, and eat out their substance. ——He has kept among us, in times of peace, Standing Armies without the Consent of our legislatures.——He has affected to render the Military independent of and superior to the Civil power.——He has combined with others to subject us to a jurisdiction foreign to our constitution, and unacknowledged by our laws; giving his Assent to their Acts of pretended Legislation:—For quartering large bodies of armed troops among us:—For protecting them, by a mock Trial, from punishment for any Murders which they should commit on the Inhabitants of these States:— For cutting off our Trade with all parts of the world:—For imposing Taxes on us without our Consent:—For depriving us in many cases, of the benefits of Trial by Jury:—For transporting us beyond Seas to be tried for pretended offenses:—For abolishing the free System of English Laws in a neighboring Province, establishing therein an Arbitrary government, and enlarging its Boundaries so as to render it at once an example and fit instrument for introducing the same absolute rule into these Colonies:—For taking away our Charters, abolishing our most valuable Laws, and altering fundamentally the Forms of our Governments:—For suspending our own Legislatures, and declaring themselves invested with power to legislate for us in all cases whatsoever.——He has abdicated Government here, by declaring us out of his Protection and waging War against us.——He has plundered our seas, ravaged our Coasts, burnt our towns, and destroyed the lives of our people.——He is at this time transporting large Armies of foreign Mercenaries to compleat the works of death, desolation and tyranny, already begun with circumstances of Cruelty & perfidy scarcely paralleled in the most barbarous ages, and totally unworthy the Head of a civilized nation.——He has constrained our fellow Citizens taken Captive on the high Seas to bear Arms against their Country, to become the executioners of their friends and Brethren, or to fall themselves by their Hands.——He has excited domestic insurrections amongst us, and has endeavoured to bring on the inhabitants of our frontiers, the merciless Indian Savages, whose known rule of warfare, is an undistinguished destruction of all ages, sexes and conditions. In every stage of these Oppressions We have Petitioned for Redress in the most humble terms: Our repeated Petitions have been answered ₒₙₗᵧ by repeated injury. A Prince whose character is thus marked by every act which may define a Tyrant, is unfit to be the ruler of a free people. Nor have We been wanting in attention to our Brittish brethren. We have warned them from time to time of attempts by their legislature to extend an unwarrantable jurisdiction over us. We have reminded them of the circumstances of our emigration and settlement here. We have appealed to their native justice and magnanimity, and we have conjured them by the ties of our common kindred to disavow these usurpations, which would inevitably interrupt our connections and correspondence. They too have been deaf to the voice of justice and of consanguinity. We must, therefore, acquiesce in the necessity, which denonunces our Separation, and hold them, as we hold the rest of mankind, Enemies in War, in Peace Friends.——

WE, THEREFORE, THE REPRESENTATIVES of the united STATES OF AMERICA, in GENERAL CONGRESS, Assembled, appealing to the Supreme Judge of the world for the rectitude of our intentions DO, in the Name, and by Authority of the good People of these Colonies, solemnly PUBLISH and DECLARE, That these United Colonies are, and of Right ought to be FREE AND INDEPENDENT STATES; that they are Absolved from all Allegiance to the British Crown, and that all political connection between them and the State of Great Britain, is and ought to be totally dissolved; and that as FREE AND INDEPENDENT STATES, They have full Power to levy War, conclude Peace, contract Alliances, establish Commerce, and to do all other Acts and Things which INDEPENDENT STATES may of right do.——AND for the support of this Declaration, with a firm reliance on the protection of divine Providence, we mutually pledge to each other our Lives, our Fortunes and our sacred Honor.

John Hancock

[*Georgia*]

Button Gwinnett
Lyman Hall
Geo Walton

[*North Carolina*]

Wm Hooper
Joseph Hewes
John Penn

[*South Carolina*]

Edward Rutledge
Thos Heyward Junr.
Thomas Lynch Junr.
Arthur Middleton

[*Maryland*]

Samuel Chase
Wm Paca
Thos Stone
Charles Carroll of
     Carrollton

[*Virginia*]

George Wythe
Richard Henry Lee
Th Jefferson

Benj^a Harrison
Thos Nelson jr.
Francis Lightfoot **Lee**
Carter Braxton

[*Pennsylvania*]

Robt Morris
Benjamin Rush
Benj^a Franklin
John Morton
Geo Clymer
Ja^s Smith.
Geo. Taylor
James Wilson
Geo. Ross

[*Delaware*]

Caesar Rodney
Geo Read
Tho M: Kean

[*New York*]

Wm Floyd
Phil. Livingston
Fran^s Lewis
Lewis Morris

The Declaration of Independence

[New Jersey]

Rich.ª Stockton
Jnº Witherspoon
Fra.ª Hopkinson
John Hart
Abra Clark

[New Hampshire]

Josiah Bartlett
W.ᵐ Whipple

[Massachusetts]

Sam¹ Adams
John Adams

Rob.ᵗ Treat Paine
Elbridge Gerry

[Rhode Island]

Step. Hopkins
William Ellery

[Connecticut]

Roger Sherman
Sam¹ Huntington
W.ᵐ Williams
Oliver Wolcott
Matthew Thornton

On the original document the signatures are arranged in six columns, by States, unnamed. Matthew Thornton of New Hampshire, the last man to sign, found no space available under William Whipple's name, therefore he added his signature to the group from Connecticut (*See endpapers*). The size of the original document is: 29⅞ inches by 24⁷⁄₁₆ inches.

Index

A

B

C

D

Index